The world is changing rapidly and this requires the church to examine the old ways and explore new ways of functioning to ensure we are relating effectively to a challenging situation. This book will help.

STUART BRISCOE
PASTOR AND AUTHOR

This is a timely book with an astonishingly wide range of current missions practices and concepts. It also has many helpful examples that can be used by missions pastors, agency leaders and missionaries. A must read for every missiologist and missions practitioner.

JIM TEBBE
URBANA DIRECTOR

Innovation in Mission excites me like no other missions book I've ever read; I came away energized and full of new ideas and possibilities. This is a must-read for mission leaders, strategic planners, and future cross-cultural kingdom workers. But let the reader beware: *Innovation in Mission* will challenge you to make significant changes in what you do and how you do it!

SCOTT MOREAU
EDITOR, EVANGELICAL MISSIONS QUARTERLY
PROFESSOR OF MISSIONS AND INTERCULTURAL STUDIES
WHEATON COLLEGE GRADUATE SCHOOL

Innovation in Mission addresses some of the most important strategic issues we face [in our rapidly changing world]. Because the global missionary movement needs to take stock of their practices, this book is important. Editors Reapsome and Hirst selected the contributors and the topics well. The chapters provide important insights for conversations that should be on the agenda of churches and missions alike. This is a book to share with others on your boards, in your Sunday school classes, and in the missions you support.

DOUG MCCONNELL
DEAN AND ASSOCIATE PROFESSOR OF LEADERSHIP, FULLER
THEOLOGICAL SEMINARY

As I read through these pages, I felt this is a book that I need to read myself. After 50 years in missions I still have much to learn.

GEORGE VERWER
FOUNDER OF OPERATION MOBILIZATION

While the standard definition of "innovation" is "The act of introducing a change or something new," the root of "innovation/innovate" comes from the concept of renewing and/or altering something already existing. What I like about the outstanding essays in this excellent book is that these missions strategists and activists are ready to take us into new, uncharted waters while maintaining the Biblical/historical maps already tested in "missiological navigation."

DR. GRANT MCCLUNG
CHURCH OF GOD WORLD MISSIONS

I've covered hundreds of missions organizations around the world. I've always wondered why someone hasn't written a book to talk about all the innovations that are having an incredible impact on missions. *Innovation in Mission* does just that. It takes innovations and trends from the church, business, short-term mission, multi-media, and more to force the reader to think outside the box and become innovators themselves in evangelism, discipleship and church planting, while reminding us of the foundations that have enabled many organizations to see incredible success over the years.

GREG YODER
EXECUTIVE DIRECTOR/ANCHOR, MISSION NETWORK NEWS

Innovation in Mission

Innovation in Mission

Insights into Practical Innovations
Creating Kingdom Impact

Edited by
Jim Reapsome and Jon Hirst

InterVarsity Press
P.O. Box 1400, Downers Grove, IL 60515-1426
World Wide Web: www.ivpress.com
Email: email@ivpress.com

© 2005 by Jim Reapsome and Jon Hirst

All rights reserved. No part of this book may be reproduced in any form without written permission from InterVarsity Press.

InterVarsity Press® is the book-publishing division of InterVarsity Christian Fellowship/USA®, a movement of students and faculty active on campus at hundreds of universities, colleges and schools of nursing in the United States of America, and a member movement of the International Fellowship of Evangelical Students. For information about local and regional activities, write Public Relations Dept., InterVarsity Christian Fellowship/USA, 6400 Schroeder Rd., P.O. Box 7895, Madison, WI 53707-7895, or visit the IVCF website at www.intervarsity.org.

All Scripture quotations, unless otherwise indicated, are taken from the Holy Bible, New International Version®. NIV®. Copyright © 1973, 1978, 1984 by International Bible Society. Used by permission of Zondervan Publishing House. All rights reserved.

Originally published by Biblica. Published in 2007 by Authentic.

Cover design: Paul Lewis
Interior design: Angela Lewis

ISBN 978-0-8308-5688-6

Printed in the United States of America ∞

 InterVarsity Press is committed to protecting the environment and to the responsible use of natural resources. As a member of Green Press Initiative we use recycled paper whenever possible. To learn more about the Green Press Initiative, visit www.greenpressinitiative.org.

Library of Congress Cataloging-in-Publication Data is available through the Library of Congress.

| P | 18 | 17 | 16 | 15 | 14 | 13 | 12 | 11 | 10 | 9 | 8 | 7 | 6 | 5 | 4 | 3 | 2 | 1 |
| Y | 28 | 27 | 26 | 25 | 24 | 23 | 22 | 21 | 20 | 19 | 18 | 17 | 16 | 15 | 14 | 13 |

Contents

Foreword		ix
Jim Plueddemann		
Preface		xiii
Jon Hirst and Jim Reapsome		
Introduction		1
Jon Hirst		

Part One: Innovation Trends

1	Innovation in Church Mobilization	9
	Ellen Livingood	
2	Innovation in Kingdom Business	25
	Joseph Vijayam	
3	Innovation in Member Care	39
	Brent Lindquist and Ah Kie Lim	
4	Innovation in Short-Term Mission	51
	Roger Peterson	
5	Innovation in Training Writers and Publishers	67
	John Maust	

Part Two: Innovation Solutions

6	Innovation in Content *Jon Hirst*	85
7	Innovation in Media Missions *Kurt Wilson*	103
8	Innovation in Strategic Planning and Partnerships *Sam Chiang*	117
9	Innovation in Resourcing Latin American Pastors *Aaron Sandoval*	131
10	Innovation in Online Learning *Joel Dylhoff*	143
11	Innovation in Theological Education in Africa *Paul Heidebrecht*	161

Conclusion

12	The Next Generation of Innovators *Jim Reapsome*	179

Notes 189

Foreword

Change is exhilarating, terrifying, and unavoidable. Jim Reapsome and Jon Hirst provide valuable insights by bringing together experts to discuss significant innovations affecting global missions. These innovations are real and are influencing the practice of missions. Missionaries, mission executives, mission pastors, and mission committees need to stay current with global changes in order to adapt strategies effectively. Whether the innovations are a help or a hindrance, a fad or a long-term trend, we need to understand them and be ready to modify programs.

Innovations are often uncomfortable. As I was stepping down as international director of SIM (Serving in Mission), a veteran missionary asked me if my successor would make as many changes as I had. She went on to say that during my tenure I had made too many changes and hoped there wouldn't be more. Another missionary often quoted, "Change and decay in all around I see" from the hymn "Abide with Me." But if the world around us is changing, our methods also need to adapt in order to fulfill the unchanging vision. Not all innovations are helpful in promoting the global cause of Christ, yet most innovations provide outstanding opportunities in ministry. For example, the Internet provides amazing opportunities for life-long learning, communication, and resources for pastors and theology students.

For ten years my wife and I traveled the SIM world, holding vision seminars. We talked about the need for programmatic change within the context of an unchanging vision. First, our leadership team solidified the SIM vision statement and core values, and then we began to reflect on massive global innovations and our need to adapt. During those ten years, the mission changed its name, merged with another mission, expanded into China, reworked the support system, and challenged sending offices to facilitate missions "from anywhere to anywhere." While vision and core values don't change, everything else is open for innovation.

As we evaluate innovation in the context of missions, it's helpful to focus on three concepts:

1. **The Unchanging Vision.** Where are we going? We need our eyes fixed on the unchanging North Star, the changeless nature of God and the unchanging vision for world missions.
2. **The Changing Situation.** Where are we? We must understand the changing world, technologies, opportunities, and resources. What are the innovations that influence our opportunities in missions?
3. **The Changing Program.** How do we get there? Mission programs must always be open to evaluation and modification. If the situation changes the program must also change. Otherwise, we will not fulfill the vision.

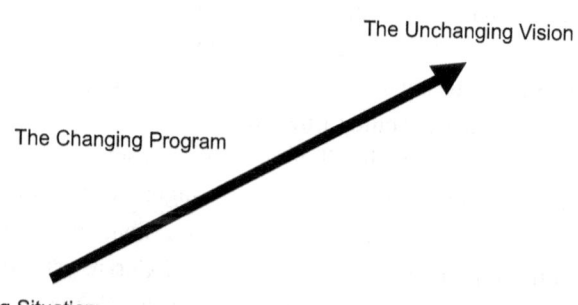

The most important things in life never change. We can take great comfort in the changeless nature of God. In this fallen world, human beings will continue to fall short of the glory of God and will be in need of Jesus Christ as their Savior. Until the Lord returns, we will always need to live by faith with an unchanging hope of eternal life in the unfailing love of the Lord. Our vision for a lost world and for a holy church will not change until the end of the age. None of these foundational convictions are fazed by developments in the digital revolution, the use of business visas, or the low cost of airfares for short-term missionaries. Heaven and earth may pass away, but the word of the Lord stands forever.

Once we rest secure in an unchanging God and an unchanging gospel, we can embrace innovation. We can seek unfolding opportunities to make whatever changes are necessary to better fulfill the vision.

I would hope that mission executives and church mission committees will reflect on *Innovation in Mission* chapter by chapter, asking if each of the innovations might be incorporated into the programs of their churches and missions. Each innovation is profound and cannot be ignored.

We don't worship innovation. So, if the innovation does not contribute to the vision, we simply move on. But neither do we worship programs. Mission institutions and church activities will be strengthened by the thoughtful application of innovative trends and solutions outlined in these pages.

JIM PLUEDDEMANN is chair of the Mission and Evangelism Department at Trinity Evangelical Divinity School. He has served as International Director of SIM and as a missionary to Nigeria. He has also served on the mission committee of his local church.

Preface
What Is Our Mandate?

With every great cause there is a mandate. Whether you join the army, become a doctor, or sit on the local school board, you must remain acutely aware of your purpose. Imagine if it weren't so and there were only rebellious soldiers, unethical doctors, and abusive public servants within a local community—the community would be greatly undermined. For a cause to succeed, its mandate must be followed.

Christianity is humanity's greatest and most noble cause, and it too has a mandate. God asks us, first, to give him glory, as stated in Psalm 106:47: "Save us, O Lord our God, and gather us from the nations, that we may **give** thanks to your holy name and **glory** in your praise." Second, God asks us to go out and share his glory with others, as expressed in Matthew 28:19: "Therefore go and **make disciples** of all nations, baptizing them in the name of the Father and of the Son and of the Holy Spirit" (emphasis added).

The mandate of a Christian is to recognize God's glory and then to obediently use personal talents to make him known to others. Missions is no more and no less. Therefore, missions is the mandate of the church and each Christ follower.

But there is little clarity around the concept of missions—and no wonder. Missions gets muddied in the waters of methodology. We are so anxious to dive into *this* strategy or *that* program that we clutter our vision and lose sight of the mandate. We also discount the methods of others because we cannot see past our own model to the greater mandate that designed both.

The great thing is that God's mandate for us to "go" is not cluttered or complex. He simply takes our willing hearts and the creativity of our minds and weaves together innovations that can only be described as revolutionary.

This book is about that mandate. You can call it whatever you like—the Great Commission, incarnational ministry, business as missions, tentmaking, preevangelism, or mercy ministries—and the list goes on and on.

Each contributor to this book has a unique experience with missions, yet, more importantly, there is one common bond—simple obedience to the mandate. This mandate was restated and reaffirmed in the Lausanne Covenant of 1974.[1] In the first article of this covenant, *The Purpose of God*, we find this statement:

> He has been calling out from the world a people for himself, and sending his people back into the world to be his servants and his witnesses, for the extension of his kingdom, the building up of Christ's body, and the glory of his name. We confess with shame that we have often denied our calling and failed in our mission, by becoming conformed to the world or by withdrawing from it. Yet we rejoice that even when borne by earthen vessels, the gospel is still a precious treasure. To the task of making that treasure known in the power of the Holy Spirit we desire to dedicate ourselves anew.

Jim Reapsome and Jon Hirst

Introduction
Jon Hirst

"To this end I labor, struggling with all his energy, which so powerfully works in me" (Colossians 1:29).

"Disturb Us, Lord"
(The Prayer of an Innovator)

Disturb us, Lord, when
we are too well pleased with ourselves,
when our dreams have come true
because we have dreamed too little,
when we arrive safely
because we have sailed too close to the shore.

Disturb us, Lord, when
with the abundance of things we possess,
we have lost our thirst for the waters of life;
having fallen in love with life,
we have ceased to dream of eternity;
and in our efforts to build a new earth,
we have allowed our vision
of the new Heaven to dim.

Disturb us, Lord, to dare more boldly,
to venture on wider seas
where storms will show your mastery;
where losing sight of land,
we shall find the stars.

We ask you to push back
the horizons of our hopes;
and to push into the future
in strength, courage, hope, and love.

Sir Frances Drake

As he looked out across the shimmering blue horizon, he saw a small fleet of cargo boats hugging the dusty Peruvian shore. You could see the gleam of victory in his eye as he tallied up the ships and imagined the riches that rested inside the hull of each Spanish ship. No men of war protected them. The Spanish never imagined that the English, or any other nation, could compete with its stranglehold on the Pacific coast of Latin America.

Sir Francis Drake had just made the boldest move against the Spanish Empire in the long history of their conflict with Great Britain. By understanding that Spain's strength came from its Andean gold, Drake crafted a plan to sail around the South American continent and attack the unprotected gold barges taking the precious cargo from Peru to Central America.

Drake took the knowledge gained from his exploits in the Caribbean, and he applied them creatively to a new situation. Throughout his career he continued to take current practices and concepts and apply them in new and creative ways. He is a great example of an innovator in naval combat.

But Drake is only one of many in a multitude of fields and domains of learning to bring about innovation. As we study progress throughout human history, we see example after example of people taking the accepted reality of the day and shoving it under a new lens. These battles, much like the battle between Jacob and the Angel of the Lord, were each a true test of character and obedience to a power greater than themselves. Many would not agree with this summary of their motivations, but, in the end, they would have to admit that all of their efforts to innovate and create came down to a yearning for a more perfect understanding of what is really true. As Christians, we know what drives that yearning in each of us.

Sir Francis Bacon in his essay "Of Innovation" clearly presents the stakes we must face. He wrote: "Surely every medicine is an innovation; and he that will not apply new remedies, must expect new evils; for time is the greatest innovator; and if time of course alter things to the worse, and wisdom and counsel shall not alter them to the better, what shall be the end?"

Without innovators who are challenging the realities of a rapidly changing world and bringing heavenly truths to the greatest challenges of the twenty-first century, we must ask the same question that Bacon asked: "What shall be the end?" Let us now set the stage for the discussions that we are about to present.

Three types of innovators have kept our modern world turning and expanding: the conceptual innovators, the pragmatic innovators, and the holistic innovators. The first type focuses on theories and concepts. You can read hundreds of doctoral dissertations in libraries around the world that showcase amazing research and conceptual innovations.

Pragmatic innovators create by applying a trusted concept in a new way in a real-life situation. These innovators do not focus their attention on writing papers and studying theories. They use experience as their main testing ground for their new ideas. Finally, holistic innovators value conceptual innovation but are steeped in the practical world of implementation. They have the capacity and patience to contemplate innovation in theory and also the position and perseverance to apply it pragmatically.

I graduated from Judson College during the rise of the dot-com years and an explosion in modern innovation. As I entered into the world of nonprofit technology, I was forced to make a decision about how I would approach my career. I could either base my decisions and actions on the trusted principles of my day or I could take the path of innovation. As I constantly reconsidered these two options, I became aware of two critical insights: (1) we cannot possibly exist in a world that does not have fundamental truths that are proven in our faith, industries, and trades; and (2) we cannot continue to develop unless those truths are being tested, molded, and contextualized for our changing world.

These two insights were not present in the dot-com exuberance that continued to produce innovations but did not have the supporting ropes of experience and truth to keep them in focus. On the other hand, many individuals and older organizations used the failure of these new-economy companies to strengthen their decision to ignore the need for innovation.

Consider the railroad companies in the United States as an example of the lack of innovation. During the 1800s the railroads represented the key travel and transportation infrastructure. They controlled most of the movement of people and goods throughout the North American continent. Then two key innovations in transportation began to occur. The first was the mass production of the automobile, which made transportation a personal and individual event instead of a corporate

Introduction

or community process. The second was the airplane, which reduced natural boundaries, decreased travel time, and made long-distance destinations practical.

Both of these innovations needed champions and investors. If the railroads had seen their role as providers of transportation solutions instead of managers of a railroad infrastructure, we might have seen Union Pacific Airlines, and the SUV might have been developed by Burlington Northern Santa Fe. But they chose not to innovate in their transportation role, and, consequently, they are mostly relegated to coal, freight, and a slice of the consumer transportation market.

As I watched some nonprofit organizations dig in their heels, refusing to change, and others run blindly into the light of change, I began to see the wisdom in what we have defined here as holistic innovation. It is a rare thing in Western culture. We tend to be a people of extremes—fundamentalists and liberals, Calvinists and Armenians, academics and pragmatists—and the list could go on.

As I realized that holistic innovation was not a common characteristic in twenty-first-century global ministry, I began to evaluate my own decisions about how I work with ministries around the world and manage strategic opportunities. I began to realize that no one was celebrating the new generation of holistic innovators who combine fundamentals with practical advances. As I looked for these unique individuals, they began to pop up everywhere. I realized that they were flying under the radar screens of the ministry world and were increasingly becoming critical players in the future of global ministry.

This book is a celebration of holistic innovation and those responsible for implementing it in the ministry community around the world. We have divided this project into two critical sections. We did this because innovation really has two major domains to consider. The first focuses on innovations in trends and significant movements of thought. The second focuses on innovations in solutions and the practical applications necessary to jump the hurdles presented by our greatest challenges. Holistic innovations must be grounded in both of these domains to have significant impact and see dynamic change. As you work through both of these sections, you will have the opportunity to differentiate between innovations in trends and innovations in solutions.

I hope that each chapter will cause you to step into new worlds and get a taste of both the theories and applications for which each of our contributors is sacrificing so much. My desire is to see these talented individuals inspire you to begin your own life of innovation that will dynamically alter your ministries forever. I pray that these innovations will breathe into each reader a new life of ingenuity, creativity, and reliance on the only One who can truly inspire our efforts.

This book is accompanied by an online tool that will allow you to continue interacting with the authors of these chapters and others about how to make innovation a reality in your organizations (see page 187).

JON HIRST is currently the Director of Communications for HCJB Global (www.hcjbglobal.org) in Colorado Springs where he is working to develop innovative strategies for communicating the Great Commission with the church world-wide. He and his wife Mindy also operate a think tank called Generous Mind (www.generousmind.com) that works with people world-wide to help them share their ideas effectively. Jon graduated from Judson College with a major in Communications and a minor in Sociology. Jon speaks often about the applications of intellectual property and content in the ministry world. Jon has had the privilege of working with a wide variety of ministries including the Baptist General Conference, the Bible League, Link Care Center, the Billy Graham Center, Tyndale House Publishers, Global Publishing Alliance (part of ECPA), SIL International, the Forum of Bible Agencies, the Seed Company, TEAM, World Bible Translation Center, and many others.

Part One: Innovation Trends

1
Innovation in Church Mobilization

Ellen Livingood

One church, infused with excitement about its involvement in missions, sends a steady stream of people to teach English classes among a largely unreached minority group in Asia and generously supports the outreach with finances and prayer. Across town, leaders of another congregation bemoan the lack of interest in missions and watch their global-outreach giving plummet.

One missionary writes off the church in North America and declares that short-term teams are a waste of time and money. Yet another cross-cultural worker in the same city enthuses about the growing partnership with a sending church and raves about the impact of short-term teams.

Involvement in cross-cultural outreach remains a biblical mandate for local churches, so what makes the difference between these congregations? Evidence shows that innovative approaches to missions mobilization—whether initiated by the church, a missionary, or mission agency—can help propel local congregations into effective global outreach. As these new methods spur involvement, they benefit the church as well as the project.

Change transforms churches' global and local environments. The makeup of many communities shifts as immigrants from around the world relocate next door. E-mail, cell phones, and inexpensive travel connect us to almost anyone, anywhere. As the speed of life increases, church schedules get tighter and volunteer hours shrink, while, at the same time, expectations for excellence in church programming and communications escalate. All of these factors and many others demand new missions approaches.

Churches Take the Initiative

Local churches are reshaping their missions programs. In many cases, the name has changed to "global outreach" or "international ministries," but the shifts go much deeper.

Sharing Who They Are

Once primarily designed for youth, short-term mission trips now are often geared for adults, families, and intergenerational groups. Field visits can ignite relationships that release tremendous potential, even from relatively small congregations.

In 1997 Guy and Kelli Caskey moved to Houston, Texas, to establish Crossroads, a network of small groups with a central celebration built on an incarnational, cell-church model with people from very diverse backgrounds. Two years later they visited Ethiopia where Caskey says, "God crushed us with a passionate burden for the nations. At first we thought maybe we were to pack up and move there, but eventually he led us to embrace a global and local vision that included Houston,

Ethiopia, and places beyond. We feel called to the nations; it's the heartbeat of all we do."

"We focus on developing relationships in which people are discipled, not running a lot of programs," Caskey explains. "And discipleship can be reproduced anywhere, although it may look different in Ethiopia than in America. Our commitment to relationships gives us an immediate connection with our brothers and sisters in Africa. We connect instantly with Ethiopians as we tell stories of how God is changing lives and building churches through believers living out the gospel, because their story-based culture predisposes them to respond to a narrative approach to presenting truth."

Partnership is an important ingredient for Crossroads. While they go to teach what they have learned from their experiences, the teams also learn much from their Ethiopian counterparts. One dynamic congregation in Addis Ababa has multiplied to about forty churches, and the pastor has spent significant time visiting Houston to learn and share.

Crossroads has also become a training ground for long-term missionaries. One missionary couple spent six months at Crossroads to experience and learn the cell model they saw being so effectively multiplied in Africa. The International Mission Board (Southern Baptist) regularly places interns there for hands-on exposure.

At least thirty people from Crossroads—one-fifth of the regular attendance—have served in Ethiopia, many of them several times. Leadership training, microenterprise development, and teaching English are key ministries. Equippers from the Houston church meet with current and prospective African equippers. Women reach out to train women.

While Caskey still shepherds the overall outreach to Ethiopia, much of the ministry happens spontaneously because the cells own the vision and each recognizes its global role. Believers in Texas and

Ethiopia have become close friends and partners. (Crossroads' website: www.xroadsonline.net.)

Working from Their DNA

Local churches are defining who they are and who they want to become by adopting vision and mission statements based on their strengths and uniqueness. Many congregations desire to apply these same qualities to their missions endeavors.

Mariners Church in southern California has been built with a creative, entrepreneurial spirit that carries over to their missions involvement. For example, the church's global outreach arm takes business people on one- and two-week trips to lead business training seminars. Putting their nine-to-five skills to work for the kingdom, Mariners' entrepreneurs teach basic business principles and Christian ethics to CEOs of everything from small, local businesses to international corporations.

As a result, a CEO Fellowship was formed that now involves over one hundred national business leaders. This group has created a "virtual foundation" that provides an avenue for funding projects that help the poor and needy.

Mariners harnesses its entrepreneurial instincts for missions in other ways. Last year their faith-challenging goal was to touch the lives of over one million people around the world through their people and resources, yet not one penny of their annual missions budget (currently over one million dollars) comes from the church budget.

Several years ago, the global outreach team set up a kiosk on Sunday mornings to sell coffee and lattes with the proceeds going to underwrite mission projects. Soon the enterprise moved into permanent quarters, extended its hours and menu, and took on the management of the church's bookstore. While directed by staff, volunteers contribute hundreds of hours for the benefit of world ministry. (Mariners' missions website: www.marinersglobal.org.)

Adopting a Strategic Focus

Church leaders are increasingly dissatisfied with the "mile-wide and inch-deep" approach that has marked the typical mission program—dozens of diverse ministries each supported with a modest amount of funds and limited congregational ownership. In growing numbers, churches are seeking one or more strategic involvements geared toward a goal they feel will have major kingdom impact. Adopting a people group, concentrating on the launch of a church-planting movement, or focusing on a specific type of ministry (such as leadership development) describes many of these concentrated efforts. For most congregations, adopting a strategic focus involves personally assessing needs and reaching out to meet them in a variety of ways.

Grace Point Church of Newtown, Pennsylvania, a suburban Philadelphia congregation of approximately six hundred, believed it could do more than just support twenty-some missionary units. Entering a major building program of their own, they wanted a partnership that would help churches in least-reached areas acquire a facility while also engaging their members in hands-on involvement. Discussions with The Evangelical Alliance Mission (TEAM), a mission agency with which they had already worked, led to an invitation to consider partnering with two church planters in the process of establishing new congregations in Japan.

Grace Point sent a survey team to Japan to meet with the missionaries, evaluate the need, and determine what they could contribute. A three-year partnership was launched with the understanding that the American church would provide a flow of short-term teams to make evangelistic contacts, an English teacher to work on-site for one to two years, and some financial assistance. The goal was to see both church plants in their own facility with a realistic mortgage, a salaried national pastor leading each congregation, and the missionaries transitioned out.

Over the course of the partnership, Grace Point sent thirty-five people to Japan, including a one-year English teacher. Several leaders from the Japanese churches visited Newtown and two groups of unbelievers from English classes were also hosted in Pennsylvania—creating opportunities to serve for those who could not travel to Japan. At the end of the project, Grace Point sent representatives to join the celebration of the opening of the second church building.

Both the American church and their missionary partners, Ron and Amy Barber, were eager to capitalize on what they had seen God do. Another partnership has been launched, this time including a mature Japanese church as the third partner in the church-planting effort.

"Trust, communication, and chemistry were critical to our success," explains Barber. "There are many benefits to this kind of close partnership, but I think they center on ownership. The partnering church can move beyond superficial contact with missionaries and missions to more significant understanding and participation. As a result, they pray differently and act differently." (Grace Point's website: www.gracepointpa.org.)

Tackling Global Issues

Some churches participate in establishing strategy or set up partnerships directly with national churches and workers. Such efforts are often led by professional missions pastors, employed by an increasing number of churches; smaller churches ignited by a big vision can also have a huge impact. In some cases, larger churches are developing contexts in which smaller congregations can maximize their involvement.

In late 2002 the missions pastors of Mars Hill Bible Church (Grand Rapids, Michigan), Perimeter Church (Atlanta, Georgia), Mariners Church (Irvine, California) and Wooddale Church (Eden Prairie, Minnesota) met in Rwanda with the HIV/AIDS crisis staring them in the eye. On that trip they sensed a call to action that has resulted in Churches Together, a new initiative to address the African AIDS pandemic.

"It is a big, audacious dream," Tom Correll of Wooddale Church admits. "But we are at least ten years behind in addressing the problem. This project is all about churches being missional, about awakening to our role as the body of Christ."

What is different about Churches Together is the commitment to direct engagement of three entities: churches in North America, churches in Africa, and mission agencies or humanitarian organizations. African churches bring the potential of a huge army of volunteers. Agencies and nongovernmental organizations can contribute the wisdom of years of experience in relief work. North American churches can offer finances and other resources. The challenge is how to connect them.

A cooperative effort of this magnitude is uncharted territory, and a multitude of questions must be answered to engage the potential partners and begin taking action. But today a growing list of churches is committed to empowering and walking beside African churches as they take the lead. Clusters of U.S. churches are working with coalitions of African churches, creating avenues for thousands of additional congregations to answer the call to make a difference. (Churches Together website: www.churchestogether.com.)

Developing Worldwide Networks

The we-they dichotomy between missionary-sending churches in the West and missionary-receiving churches in Africa, Asia, and Latin America is fast dissolving as local congregations discover a kinship regardless of where they are located. Sister-church relationships are multiplying with benefits flowing in both directions. While this may be a fairly simple reciprocal relationship between two congregations, some churches are developing worldwide networks.

Elmbrook Church in Milwaukee, Wisconsin, is pioneering a new venture called the Global Church Partnership. Challenged by the emergence of high-impact churches in strategic cities around the world, Elmbrook has launched a global network with the La Puerta Abierta Church in Buenos Aires, Argentina; the Nairobi (Kenya) Chapel; and the Glenabbey Church of Belfast, Northern Ireland; and will likely add a few others.

The four churches share a commitment not only to global outreach but also to culturally expressive worship and to strong, biblical exposition. The essence of the network is high-trust relationships. Each church encourages the others by sharing its cultural uniqueness in worship, by ministering in reciprocal relationships, and by jointly conceiving ways to further the local and global impact of each congregation.

The cooperative effort is proceeding slowly as relationships develop and is not Western driven. Annually, each network partner sends three or four members to a meeting held at one of the churches. The willingness to invest time and money just to come together is considered critical. Recently, a joint mission venture in Argentina involved young adults from each congregation. Another joint team is being considered to minister in Uganda, and a conference on worship in eastern Congo is on the drawing board.

Staff exchanges and shared internships are strengthening the ties. One couple from Elmbrook served for three years on the staff of the Nairobi Chapel, and another couple is now doing the same. Interns from Belfast and Nairobi have come on short-term assignments to Milwaukee. The teaching pastors of the network have preached in each other's pulpits.

"Our network revolves around the value of sharing what each member brings," Dick Robinson emphasizes. "For example, the African church has much to teach us about the gift of suffering. And we are learning about prayer and worship from our global partners. Mutuality and reciprocity are the keys to success." (Elmbrook's missions website: www.elmbrook.org/harvest.)

Agencies Take the Initiative

While initially hesitant about these new church initiatives, mission agencies are increasingly eager to explore new models of partnering with churches. Wrestling through questions of control, competence, and financing, agencies are discovering that true partnerships take work but also multiply results.

Helping Churches Plant Churches

Focused historically around the work of long-term missionaries, agencies sometimes struggle to use short-term personnel. But some have developed highly effective programs.

The e3 Partners Ministry (formerly Global Missions Fellowship) creates dynamic synergy by pairing teams of North American Christians with a national church in places like Russia and Colombia. The result after one week of concentrated evangelism was one—or, more often, three to five—embryonic new church that will be nurtured to maturity by the partnering national church after the North Americans leave.

The e3 staff lay the groundwork with the North American church participants by meeting with the pastor and other church leaders and then presenting the challenge to the congregation. The e3's church mobilization director, Dana Crawford, lauds the commitment of the associate staff—volunteers with extensive training and experience as trip leaders who contribute their time to work with churches and brief team participants and to lead at least one or two mission trips each year.

Team members are trained through a series of self-studies enhanced with video presentations and a final orientation at a central site or by phone. Once on location overseas, each North American is matched with a national believer and a translator, if one is needed. Throughout the week of ministry, the visitors transfer their evangelism skills and passion to their national partners. In the process, teams see people come to Christ and gathered into small house groups or churches.

The key to long-term results is the commitment of the national church partner to investing time and effort to preserve the harvest. The e3 Partners Ministry looks for churches that share their vision and have enough people to follow up the new believers and provide pastoral leadership for new congregations.

This innovative approach offers a win-win situation for both partners. When trained to use simple evangelism tools, believers from both cultures get excited to see how God uses them and want to continue to share the gospel in their own context. Both churches are challenged to focus on a strategic goal—to trust God to bring a church into existence and to continue a long-term relationship with the new group of believers.

While e3 Partners has no overall statistics on how many of these church plants survive, they regularly receive updates. One such update was from a Southern Baptist missionary in Colombia who reported that all ten of the new works started during campaigns in 2000 were still functioning three years later with an average attendance of thirty-two adults and seventy-six children. (e3 Partners' website: www.e3partners.org.)

When Daniel Holmquist became pastor in 1999, the Lancaster (California) Evangelical Free Church (LEFC) was a congregation of just fifty people with token missions involvement. But this small church became convinced they didn't have to be large in order to make a global difference. All but one of the elders joined e3 staffer Dan Hitzhusen on LEFC's initial short-term team committed to high-impact evangelism in South Asia.

That first team saw five new congregations planted, and LEFC has never looked back. After watching God use them on multiple e3 trips to various areas of the world, the congregation adopted a people group in East Asia and now sends teams there approximately every nine months. An estimated 60 percent of LEFC adults have been on one of these trips, which Hitzhusen describes as "discipleship on steroids" for their impact on the lives of those who go.

"Everybody goes on every trip," Holmquist declares. "By that we mean everyone goes spiritually and provides assistance and support. For example, children make bracelets that present the gospel through different colored beads that are used by the teams in outreach. Everyone is encouraged to sign up for the twenty-four-hour prayer chain or the fasting chain. And people adopt team members, committing to help care for their families while they are gone."

Holmquist also has watched his congregation learn to "pray large"—asking God to do more of the miraculous things they have seen him accomplish through them in tough circumstances around the world. When teams return, the church holds a story night, often taking three hours to allow people to describe how God blessed their involvement and answered prayer.

Now numbering one hundred and fifty in attendance, LEFC is on target in fulfilling its goal of fielding one new long-term missionary unit every two years. And their long- and short-term ministries involve them in partnerships spanning the globe as they network with multiple agencies and other churches from California to Singapore.

LEFC does not have a mission committee. Instead, missions is led by the elders and integrated into the heart of everything the congregation does. "Missions has given our church an identity," Holmquist declares. "To know you are being used by God to reach people who have never heard the gospel is incredibly energizing." (LEFC's website: www.lancasterefc.org.)

Giving Away the Task

Some mission agencies are actively encouraging local churches to take ownership of aspects of global outreach. Welcoming church initiative, they shift from CEO to consultant in the missions enterprise.

Innovation in Mission

As director of the mission responders network for the Lutheran Church Missouri Synod (LCMS) World Mission, Steve Hughey wrestled with how to involve Lutheran congregations in global outreach. He began to experiment with partnerships that allowed congregations and smaller mission societies to take ownership of the task. In 1996 he brought together representatives from twelve societies for sharing, and from that meeting came the Association of Lutheran Mission Agencies (ALMA) that now includes eighty-seven of the over one hundred separate mission agencies in the LCMS. (The ALMA website: www.almanetwork.org.)

Individual churches or groups of churches are encouraged to consider mission needs, discover where God wants to use them, and then form their own mission society complete with registration as a not-for-profit organization. Hughey shares information with the new groups to help them learn from others and puts them in touch with the appropriate ALMA groups for assistance with issues such as funding, communication, and strategic planning. ALMA groups meet together annually along with LCMS World Mission staff and missionaries to coordinate their efforts.

Many of these societies then develop a formal partnership with LCMS World Mission with a written agreement that defines responsibilities, explains relationships, and clarifies accountability. They work with the missionaries and field directors to set strategy, whereas, deploying career missionaries is usually left up to the LCMS World Mission. The societies field short-term volunteers, provide services, and supply materials and money for the work. For example, one entity called Orphan Grain Train ships mission supplies for various groups. People of the Book Lutheran Outreach is coordinating a new church-planting effort for Pakistan in cooperation with ten other ALMA mission agencies as well as LCMS World Mission.

A variety of strategic partnerships are offered as options for Lutheran congregations and mission societies. Five levels are offered from basic project or missionary support to initiation of work among an unreached group where the denomination has never before ministered.

Hughey observes, "This is a great way to both reach more lost people and involve the people of God in meaningful ways. It is a real win-win in that it avoids a 'them and us' mentality." (The LCMS World Mission website: www.mission.lcms.org.)

Serving Global-Local Outreach

Once typically referred to as *foreign* mission societies, agencies today are coming to recognize that their expertise in reaching across cultural and religious boundaries is of great value in helping churches reach immigrants in their own communities.

After a century of operation as a foreign mission, Serving in Mission (SIM) began to apply its expertise to reach ethnic communities in North America. In 2000 SIM added an Ethnic Focus division designed to mobilize and equip churches to reach the burgeoning ethnic populations at their door, under the direction of Gerry Johnson, former SIM church planter in Eritrea.

Their services fall into three categories. First, they offer feasibility and evaluation studies to local congregations considering the launch of an ethnic ministry. They talk to the pastoral staff, lay leaders, and any ethnic believers within the church. Their critique not only assesses the church's potential but also predicts problems they will face and suggests practical steps for initiating an ethnic ministry in that particular location.

Second, SIM Ethnic Focus team members offer to pastors seminars on ethnic ministry. These one-day programs highlight models of successful church-based ethnic ministry and present guidelines for mentoring such ministries and how-tos for getting started. Similar one-day seminars focus on ministry to particular ethnic groups or specialized outreaches such as international student ministry or English Second Language tutor training.

Third, and perhaps most importantly, the SIM team provides ongoing church mentoring, coming alongside to walk a church through the process of starting ethnic outreach. Their guidance covers topics such as choosing an organizational model for ethnic ministry that fits the church's ministry context, how to prepare the congregation, tips on becoming more "internationals friendly," training for English language teachers, suggestions on how to advertise English classes, and networking with similar ministries elsewhere. There is a waiting list of churches who want this kind of assistance. (SIM's website: www.sim.org.)

Currently, the Ethnic Focus team consists of sixty people, primarily former SIM missionaries, many with expertise in a particular religion or people group or a specific type of ministry. One church they have assisted is Maranatha Chapel in Evergreen Park, just outside Chicago.

When former missionary Doug Banks accepted the call to pastor this Caucasian congregation, it was with the agreement that the church would reach out to the large ethnic communities surrounding them. Within a ten-minute drive of the church were thousands of Eastern Europeans, Hispanics, Arabs, and African Americans.

Initially, church members were supportive but a bit apprehensive. SIM personnel helped explain the concept and offered hints on preparing the congregation. They provided guidelines on doing demographic studies and suggested resources on sharing the gospel with Muslims.

As he prayed for God's vision for this congregation of just over three hundred people, Banks felt led to outline a five-year plan that included the launch of a new ethnic congregation each year. Maranatha already has added a Hispanic congregation numbering about eighty people and an Arabic-language group that has climbed to an average of forty in attendance.

Banks likes to describe it as "one church with three congregations." There is a unified pastoral staff, board, and budget, but each group holds its own weekly worship services with occasional tri-lingual services. They also meet together for baptisms and missions conventions.

During the summer Maranatha holds International Sunday Nights at the Park, featuring potluck suppers that resemble an international buffet. Each week the congregations take turns providing dessert, music, and a devotional, introducing the others to their culture. Games and activities create a setting for fellowship that melds people from different backgrounds and also attracts passersby. One evening a group of curious young Arabs approached the group, and a member of the Arab congregation was able to share his faith with them. On Wednesday evenings the church holds a unified prayer service that includes teaching, worship, and prayer. Interceding together has brought the three congregations even closer.

The early hesitations of the original congregation have evaporated. Now they work side by side with their Hispanic and Arab fellow believers in vacation Bible school and rejoice together over God's blessings to Maranatha—such as the news that a Muslim recently placed his faith in Christ. (Maranatha Chapel's website: www.mchapel.net.)

Some Questions Demand Consideration

Churches, missionaries, and mission agencies open to innovation have vast opportunities to plow new ground. As new methods are considered, important questions demand consideration:

- From a biblical perspective, who owns the task? The local church? The missionary? The agency? All of them? None of them?
- Which party should take the lead? Why?
- Do we have a kingdom mentality, or are we, perhaps unconsciously, focused on benefiting our own organization?

- How do we make a clear-eyed assessment of what we bring to the task?
- Are we sensitive to the priorities of the national churches around the world and sufficiently appreciative of their current and potential contributions?
- Have we embraced the fact that the mission field is no longer foreign but local as well as global?
- Are we willing to take risks and adopt new approaches, especially as younger generations move into roles of service and leadership?

ELLEN LIVINGOOD was born and raised in Lancaster County, Pennsylvania, and enjoyed the privilege of a Christian home. She is a graduate of Philadelphia Biblical University and Wheaton Graduate School. Her ministry experience includes a short-term mission assignment in France and service with a local church, Bible college, and two mission agencies. In 2005 she launched Catalyst Services to assist mission agencies to collaborate more effectively with local churches. Ellen is also director of Global Outreach at Grace Point Church of Newtown, Pennsylvania.

2
Innovation in Kingdom Business

Joseph Vijayam

Business may be broadly defined as the production and distribution of goods and services that are needed for life. "Kingdom business" is a deliberate equivocation that refers to two ideas. The first is the business of God's kingdom (Luke 2:49), or Christian ministry, which seeks to disciple individuals, nations, and people groups for eternal life in the kingdom here and hereafter. The second, narrower meaning of kingdom business as used in this chapter is a commercial business whose explicit goal and *raison d'etre* are to serve God's kingdom concerns. I am the chief executive and part owner of an information technology business called Olive Technology, which seeks to fulfill this concept. This business model will be described in this chapter.

Changing Equations between Business and Mission

The industrial age has changed the character and structure of business and social life. The net result of this change, for the purpose of my thesis, is that life has become relatively secularized and compartmentalized. Religion has less access to the various departments of life and groups of people. Religion is relatively isolated from life in general. While it is true that people need God today as much as ever, their need is addressed less often than it was before the advent of modernization.

New forms of mission work have, in God's providence, arisen in response to the changing situation. Businesspeople going into missions is one of many such initiatives.

To understand the changing equations between mission and business, let us look at some relevant aspects of the complex changeover to modernity. What I write applies primarily to the developed countries, and it also applies to the others in so far as they too have joined the march of globalization, leaving them no choice other than to modernize.

Until the end of the medieval age, religion was woven into the fabric of the local community and culture. Most people were engaged in trades relating to the basic necessities of life, such as food and clothing for the subsistence of the family and a limited local community. Trade beyond the boundaries of the local community was minimal and of limited significance to the lives of most people. With the agricultural-industrial-technological revolution came cheaper mass production for the competitive market. An explosive growth of international trade, combined with recent strides in telecommunication and information technology, has given rise to the global village.

Another relevant aspect of the change was specialization in work, a shift away from basic necessities to numerous new products and services creating new trades and new fractured social groupings. Simultaneously, this led to the weakening of traditional local communities and to the religious and cultural roots and nurture they supplied to individuals and families. This process was accentuated by the migration of people to urban industrial and educational centers, which marginalized and secularized many people.

Mass literacy was another important development that affected religion. On the one hand, this brought religion to the people and facilitated mission outreach. On the other hand, however, with the wide acceptance of naturalistic, evolutionary thought, it undergirded the secularization of life. Along with this came the sexual revolution, challenging the hardiest of social institutions, the family. Religion and church fellowship, once an integral part of social and family life, is today more a matter of individual choice.

Missionary Responses

Among numerous responses of the church to the modern situation, I mention a few by way of illustration. Overseas missions was one of the earliest responses of the church to the changed situation. This was a revival of the apostolic model of evangelism. Like Paul and Thomas, many missionaries such as William Carey, the Moravian missionaries, and the Swiss Basel Mission adopted the self-supporting, or tentmaking strategy, but with one difference that anticipates the modern businessperson's approach.[1]

While Paul, a hunted and persecuted missionary, could not attempt more than poverty relief, these missionaries established businesses that contributed to economic development of whole societies and even nations. The Moravian missionaries of the eighteenth century contributed significantly to the development of some islands of the West Indies by founding industries run on Christian principles. The Swiss Basel Mission, a tentmaking missionary society, laid the foundations of the economy of modern Ghana.

Educational and medical missions made modern science and technology available to the needy in many backward areas and set stan-

Innovation in Mission

dards of excellence in those societies. The Christian Medical College and Hospital in Vellore, India, founded by Ida Scudder, is known to be among the best healthcare institutions in Asia. The Madras Christian College founded by Scottish missionaries continues strong in India to this day.

Missions oriented to specific social strata and groups was another recent development. Examples of this are the Zenana Mission, which targets secluded upper-caste women in India and the Pandita Ramabai Mukti Mission, which works with child widows in India. Various agencies focus on children, youth, and the elderly. Counseling ministries, especially family counseling, are another specialized modern ministry. The use of new media to reach large numbers of people has been another new thrust.

Businesspeople in Missions

By all of these new missions, and others, more people are being won for Christ than ever before, and there has been unprecedented growth of the church in Asia and Africa. South Africa, the Philippines, Singapore, and several African countries are fast turning into predominantly Christian nations. But there are segments of society and regions of the world that are hardly accessible even to the kind of specialized ministries mentioned above. Christian businesspeople and professionals can help reach such individuals.

Two types of these individuals require special mention. First, there are the secularized and busy professionals in the West who have never encountered the gospel and tend to ignore it as a superstition. The lives of Christian colleagues are the only gospel they are ever likely to read. Second, 70 percent of countries, excluding the West, restrict or exclude professional evangelism, especially by foreign missionaries. But tentmaker professionals and businesspeople in suitable developmental undertakings still have access to individuals in such countries. While there is a resurgence of extremist religious nationalism in Hindu and

Islamic countries, many people in these countries would be more open to the gospel if only they could see a convincing practical version of it. Many Christians in businesses and professions are responding to the challenges. But the response is still a small stream, whereas, mighty rivers are needed.

There are several ways in which Christians in business and secular professions have responded to this opportunity and need: (1) witnessing in the workplace, (2) witnessing in the marketplace, (3) using business as mission, (4) tentmaking, and (5) initiating kingdom business. Kingdom business is my focus. It can, in principle, include all the others, and so it is helpful to look at the other four first. These are not mutually exclusive approaches, and the titles assigned to them are nothing more than convenient tags.

Witnessing in the Workplace

This simply means witnessing to colleagues. Here is an example from George Samuel. Samuel is now based in Kerala, India, as a full-time evangelist. Formerly, he worked in the United States as a nuclear-medicine scientist. His son, Johnny, a handicapped boy whom he loved dearly, died in his hometown in India, and Samuel received the news while abroad. Soon after, a North American man who was an acquaintance called him and started sharing with him some personal problems. This friend knew nothing about Samuel's bereavement. Samuel, with his characteristic kindness and gentleness, listened, sympathized, comforted, and counseled him. Toward the end of the conversation, the friend discovered that Samuel had just lost his son. He was deeply moved. "I am griping about my little problems, and you who have lost your son are listening to me and helping me without any complaints!" he exclaimed. The man put his trust in God, and his life turned around. That was not all. A few dozen scientist colleagues of Samuel, who were impressed by the peace and spontaneous kindness that filled Samuel in his grief, came to Christ. They saw Samuel's life and learned what the Christian faith can supply, which science does not.

In the workplace, witnessing cannot be as primarily verbal as it can be in church, since the workplace is where people meet in their professional roles.

Witnessing in the Marketplace

This is a matter of witnessing to the customer and the supplier in the marketplace. Once again, the principle of witnessing through one's life holds good. But there is a special problem that requires mention: the obvious conflict of financial interests between the businessperson and the customer or supplier that tempts the former to be less than fair or kind. That honesty is the best policy is now standard thinking in business theory, at any rate, in the West.

Here is a typical story from my own experience. In the first year of the inception of my business with just four employees, we were struggling to survive. Then a government agent came with an offer of a half-million-dollar dream project. I praised God, accepted it gladly, and booked my ticket to go abroad to buy the needed software tools. Then surfaced a table of kickbacks that we should pay to all those involved on the government side of the contract, right down to the government minister. This still left an ample profit margin for the business. Seeing my reluctance, the agent pitied my youthful ignorance of normal business routine and sought my father's help to persuade me. Obviously, we declined after explaining the reason for our stand on the issue. How could my father have reached the position he had without using such methods? he argued. If my father and I had accepted his proposition, my business would have stabilized immediately, but not as a kingdom business, not as one that has God's blessing on it. The growth that God in his faithfulness gave us subsequently reminds me of Tolstoy's famous maxim, "God sees the truth, but waits"—and I guess we have to wait too.

Tentmaking

There is some uncertainty about the coverage of the term *tentmaking*. In the literature on the subject, a tentmaker is typically defined as someone who finds placement in a restricted-access foreign culture as a secular worker with the object of sharing the gospel. The "Tentmakers Roundtable Conference of Hyderabad" (India, 1989) considered this definition too narrow because it excludes the apostle Paul himself and his associates in Corinth, Apollo and Priscilla. The conference defined a tentmaker as either *(a)* a missionary like Paul, who goes into business for partial or full self-support; or *(b)* a secular worker like Apollo or Priscilla in Corinth, who expends considerable time for ministry.

The conference thought that in addition to evangelism, a goal of the tentmaker is, after the example of Paul, relief of poverty and, in the modern context, economic development of the poor. I take the cross-cultural tentmaker of type *(a)* as being a subset of type *(b)*, a secular worker who doubles as a missionary.

My concern is with secular workers who engage in mission. They help to penetrate sociocultural or political barriers to the gospel. They also help take the gospel across what may be called the poverty barrier. A great example is the late bullock-cart evangelist and bishop of the Church of South India, Bunyan Joseph. In the 1930s people around him lived in abysmal poverty, most of them eating less than one rice-gruel meal a day. Recall Gandhi's famous saying, "To the hungry man, bread is God." Bunyan Joseph not only supported himself by means of simple contextual technologies, but taught the same to the poorest and helped meet their physical needs in this way. In the process he gave them both bread for the body and the Bread of Life. The model he created has launched a contextual technology-cum-evangelism movement in India through the work of TENT. Its main projects are Joshua Vision India and Indian Women in Lord's Labor, founded by my father, B.E. Vijayam. It is a perfect fit for me to be the chief executive of a ministry that promotes tentmaking because I follow the same model.

Business as Ministry

There are some businesses that fit the mold of a ministry by virtue of what they do, depending on their product or service. They could be labeled either way. Those involved in such work are said to be employed in "noble professions." Examples of such businesses are education, health care, child care, and so on, which can be profit-making businesses and, at the same time, be a ministry. An outstanding example of this is a business owned by a Christian brother whom I know, who runs dozens of educational institutions in India. Though the business is one that generates good profits, these institutions are introducing its staff and pupils to the gospel message. This model, followed by many Christians in India, has been so successful that it is now being imitated by some Hindus to propagate their religion.

Kingdom Business

The problem with the secular worker going into missions is that, typically, he or she is someone else's employee, and the fact remains that no one can serve two masters. In this connection, the "Tentmakers Roundtable Conference of Hyderabad," referred to above, made a significant distinction between self-employed tentmakers and the other-employed ones. The great advantage of kingdom business is that the businesspeople concerned are self-employed within limits, somewhat like missionary doctors, engaged in what I referred to earlier as business as ministry. What then is the difference? The difference is a matter of the starting point. The missionary starts at the mission end of the spectrum and goes into business; the businessperson starts at the business end and goes into mission. Their constituencies differ and, possibly, their business and mission strategies. The world sees the first as a missionary and the second as a businessperson, but they are the same within. The results can be similar, whichever end one starts from.

The main purpose of most businesses is defined as the maximization of shareholder wealth. In a kingdom business, the main purpose is to expand the kingdom of God. Profits and an increase of shareholder wealth (which also ought to be ploughed back into kingdom work) are byproducts. Profits are essential for survival of any business. But they need not become the very purpose for existence. My business is built on this principle. It has already proved to be something of a successful model in commercial terms. We have also seen some significant results in mission work within seven years since its founding. The internal mission statement of the company is to provide human, technological, and financial resources to grow God's kingdom in India and worldwide. Besides supporting various mission endeavors, the company engages in assisting ministries through technology tools and services, through transferring technical skills and knowledge at conferences on technology, and finally through an evangelistic website targeting urban youth.

Before I outline the characteristics and challenges of kingdom business, here is how I stumbled into it, by God's merciful design and guidance. Under my father's guidance and encouragement, I took my first step, as a teenager, to plan my life and set my goals. I decided to serve the Lord and promote the gospel among the needy in India as a tentmaker. After completing my academic education overseas, I returned to my homeland to be a tentmaker, forsaking a more comfortable and promising future in the West. Against the advice of others to take a job with some renowned multinational company in India, I decided to take a job in a fledgling company. I expected more flexible work hours, after stipulating a five-day week and limited office hours, but in God's providence, it did not work out. It was only after I left that job, waited on the Lord in prayer, and risked my livelihood that a new door opened to start a business in a small and humble manner.

There are several ingredients that go into making a kingdom business. First, the founding members should be committed Christians who are faithful to God. They must be committed to a common kingdom-oriented vision, not only in general abstract terms but also in concrete objectives that involve the business. I am fortunate to have such men and women of God on my board and management team.

Second, the leader or CEO of the business should see his or her role as primarily being a missionary in the marketplace and secondarily as a businessperson. The intention should be distinct (in philosophy) and distinguishable (in practice) from that of the typical businessperson.

Third, there must be a continual emphasis on the business being a ministry as well as a business, rather than one or the other. This has to be done at all levels, beginning with the board room and extending to the hiring practices of the company. Priority must be given to excellence, integrity, fairness, honesty, and concern for people as people, over growth, profits, and efficiency. The latter will follow when kingdom values are followed. The world is beginning to realize and appreciate this truth, according to the record-breaking sales of popular business literature recommending such values as the best practices in the marketplace.

A recent example from my own experience explains how we are sometimes required to choose a less-efficient or unprofitable option that defies conventional wisdom but follows the path of the kingdom. The company accountant, a high-caste orthodox Hindu, became ill with what appeared to be an incurable condition of the liver that was rapidly deteriorating. The situation seemed so bad that he was not expected to return to his job, let alone return quickly. I had to decide whether a substitute should replace the accountant to ensure smooth running of the company or whether an appeal should be sent to the board members, management, and staff to pray for the accountant's recovery and have the company pay in part for the costs of treatment. The latter was done. God answered with a miraculous and almost instantaneous healing of the accountant. Not only does this likely ensure a much smoother operation of the accounting department than finding a quick substitute but it also has the potential of adding one or more souls to the kingdom. The accountant's mother is already a new believer, and he and his wife are coming closer to Jesus.

Characteristics of a Kingdom Business

Based on my own experience, listed below are the characteristics of a kingdom business:

- It is something unique that God plans and calls one to, in his own way.
- "His kingdom first" decisions on our part are required before God can lead us into his highest will for him. Mature Christian leaders tell me that unselfish, risky decisions taken early in life often set the course of a person's life and ministry.
- A life partner and business partners or shareholders must share in the same vision. There should be no question of being unequally yoked with shareholders who are seeking personal gain in preference to kingdom gain.
- Profits should be plowed back into ministry in the first place; and second, into business development not undertaken for its own sake but to serve business-cum-mission services.
- A kingdom business should undertake mission tasks separate from profit.
- In a kingdom business riddles are solved by prayer and by God's power. No business can survive without making adequate profit. Conflicts are bound to arise between the business requirements of economy and profit making on the one side and Christian ethic, love, and public interest on the other. It is difficult to decide how far to forgive an erring or inefficient employee or keep sick employees in order to build them up and train them at the expense of immediate profit and economy. No rule can yield an answer, but God's guidance should be sought

and his power tapped by prayer and faith. But no one can prescribe how much faith others should have in their personal and professional situation. All have been given a measure of faith, which is for them to discover honestly and to develop (Romans 12:3–8).

- The very term kingdom business has built into it a conflict between kingdom interests and business interests in our imperfect world. Such conflicts happen in the free world when a business cannot survive without serving unethical market demands or in totalitarian countries where a business cannot run without compromising faith and mission. If the conflict becomes irresolvable, the kingdom business partners should know where their choice lies and count the cost in anticipation.

Application Steps

The steps outlined below are lessons from the story told above and my description of kingdom business:

- Set goals according to the principle, "Seek first his kingdom and his righteousness, and all these things will be given to you as well" (Matthew 6:33).

- Wait on God for guidance into a business ministry of his choice.

- Allow God to choose life and business partners who identify with the founder's God-given vision and mission objectives.

- Plow back profits into mission and business in the same way, under God's guidance.

- Be committed to the development of your employees, partners, suppliers, and customers, all as God's children, and to public interest.

- According to ability, undertake kingdom tasks that bring no profit in commercial terms.
- Resolve inevitable conflicts between business and kingdom interests through prayer and faith, according to the measure of faith imparted by God.
- If the conflict between kingdom commitments and business interests become irresolvable, count the cost in advance and resolve to choose the kingdom.

JOSEPH VIJAYAM is founder and president of a software company, Olive Technology, with offices in India and the United States. His company supports the work of 3i, TENT, and other ministries in India with leadership development and high-end technology. He serves on the boards of several Christian organizations in India and the United States. After completing undergraduate and graduate studies in computer science and business administration, he returned to India to fulfill his vision of being a tentmaker.

3
Innovation in Member Care
Brent Lindquist and Ah Kie Lim

In the broadest sense, member care describes what a mission organization does to care for its members. This includes seminars and conferences, counseling or pastoral care, and reading materials and workbooks. Most North American mission organizations have either a partial or organization-wide strategy for member care in effect. In the developing world, these things are largely ideals. Much of their implementation is either waiting to happen or in the initial stages of development.

While North American-based organizations may be farther along in caring for their members, their care tends to be narrowly focused on counseling-related individual or family strategies, as opposed to being broadly focused on human resource-related organizational strategies.

In this chapter we will attempt to illustrate some of the relevant issues we have managed as we have begun to apply a holistic model of member care to mission organizations in the new sending countries

(NSCs). These are countries that have, until recently, been the focus of the old sending countries of North America and Europe. NSCs include countries in Latin America, Asia, and Africa.

I (Brent Lindquist) lead one of the oldest and largest counseling and pastoral care-focused member care organizations in North America. I have been working with Ah Kie Lim in refining member care strategies for the NSCs. She is Malaysian by nationality and has worked as a pastoral member care provider and manager in a South Asian context for over ten years. We came together because of our concern that more needs to be done in NSCs than merely to generically apply the member care contexts from North America.

We need to evaluate the *caring technology* to see how it may fit with the South Asian context. While it can be said that people are similar in many ways, we are concerned with the subtle differences in service and treatment definitions, cultural attitudes, and the role of the various participants—including the mission organization, the local church, and the family. We need to develop specific arenas of care for this specific population.

Our concerns are similar to those expressed in this statement by Belinda Ng: "As Asian churches take up the challenge of missions, they are gradually facing the same problems that churches in the First World have experienced. Attrition, discouragement, sending the wrong kind of missionaries, discontentment, disillusionment, and many other categories of negative feelings are now surfacing and creating concerns. Pastoral care (member care) is often an after-thought, rather than part of the strategy at the outset of a church mission program. Financial and material supports are usually the main concerns, because they are more obvious and visible. Yet the thrust is that, just like professional people at home needing some pastoral care, missionaries need the same generic care."[1]

We need to exercise caution in selecting member care technology. And more than just *what* we use, we need to decide *how* and, very importantly, *when* to apply it. We must be sure the proper foundations of member care are in place before applying the selected technology. In some cases, we have discovered significant innovations through foundation building. Some notable efforts have been made to help the NSCs with the fundamentals of member care, such as those mentioned in Kelly O'Donnell's edited book, *Doing Member Care Well*.[2] This compendium includes numerous international authors. However, many of their references are taken from the former sending-country frame of reference. We look forward to the day when the NSC people reference their own writers and resources.

In the meantime, how do we work together to develop a more contextualized or indigenous model for specific issues within specific populations? We do not have a complete answer, and it will take years to see if our efforts will bear fruit. What follows is a review of the issues in their present state of development. It should be pointed out that we are not saying that we have been responsible for all the indicated issues. Although we have been involved with some of them from the beginning, others have risen out of the milieu of doing mission work in a South Asian context. We are indebted to those many pioneers from other organizations who have been part of this process.

Foundations of Member Care

Nothing arises in a vacuum. Ideas come out of specific historical, cultural, and organizational milieus. This is certainly the case with member care. At great risk of being overly simplistic, member care arose out of a Western mission organizational context, or out of a reaction to it. Following World War II the United States, as well as most Western countries, saw the proliferation of mental health-based treatments of cultural and psychological conditions. This spread to the churches where the therapist has come alongside the pastor to care for the flock.

Mission organizations, chronically underfunded, tended to have a default attitude about caring for their people. In the best sense, this allowed for people to depend on God for supplying daily needs. In the worst sense, this allowed benign neglect to replace intentional care and planning. Sometimes the old adage of "If it works, don't fix it" gets changed to "Don't look too closely to see if it works well or not." Over the last forty years in North America, numerous organizations have risen to address the training and care needs of North American missionaries. These efforts have gone a long way toward helping missionaries be more effective. However, a large number of the programs are counselor-based in outlook. That is, they were often formed in reaction to a perceived need of counseling resulting from pain or pathology.

Since the mission organizations generally had no funds to do their own member care work, their efforts at member care typically fell into the area of personnel or pastoral care, leaving the more intense care to professionals. This bifurcation is similar to the North American model of establishing a boundary between general, peer-based counseling and professional counseling. The well-meaning and successful pioneers in member care in North America are to be applauded. But as we looked at the underdeveloped NSC environments, we asked ourselves if this was necessarily the best culturally-relevant model to follow. We also looked at whether this was the best place to start. It wasn't.

What is the state of member care in South Asian missions? Our first observation is that member care is viewed with skepticism and suspicion. Asian churches and mission organizations have sometimes expressed the fear that too much care from them will spoil their missionaries, or the mission endeavor will not be cost effective. Some believe that missionaries should be willing to suffer all for Jesus, for the sake of carrying the gospel.

There is an Asian movement that seeks to send people into the worst conditions with minimal outside resources or care. "There are others that believe too much care can become a distraction and ultimately make workers less resilient and effective."³ Because of this, Asian churches and missions organizations are very cautious when giving care to their missionaries.

Missionaries who really need care are afraid to ask for it because they could be branded as not sacrificial in their ministry or, even worse, not fit to be on the mission field. Often they live with unmet needs and suffer disappointments with their mission organizations or sending churches because they are afraid to seek help. There is also a real sense of ambivalence about psychology, psychological counseling, mental health and illness, and other labels more acceptable in the West. This ambivalence is also based on financial issues as well. The traditional models of care from the West are mostly out of bounds financially for South Asians.

The more basic issue about where to start member care development is where the mission organizations are in terms of holistic-care models. Mission organizations may not have even started planning for health-related concerns, let alone personnel or member care issues. They also may not have a solid financial base to do much of substance. Therefore, when we looked at developing member care in this context, we had to start earlier in the developmental process than we would have with most Western organizations. Although this book is about innovations, our innovations may look as though we are going the other way—back to the basics.

Member Care Issues and Innovative Responses

A number of critical issues arise from various practical situations on the field. In this section we want to mention and illustrate these issues and then show some of the innovative responses to them. Excellent member care requires that we press on beyond what are usually considered purely spiritual issues and tackle important matters like financial needs, health care needs, and savings and pension programs.

Financial Needs

"My wife has been sick for two years and we do not have enough money for her to seek better treatment. We barely have enough monthly financial support to meet our family needs," says one missionary. Some missionaries do not have enough money to travel to their ministry locations if they are working in several villages. "In many of the prayer meetings, the missionaries pray for their financial needs to be met. If they wait for all their needs to be met, India and the world would never be reached with the gospel."[4]

Generally, missionaries take the step of faith and trust God to meet all their needs. Does this mean that the mission agencies do not need to meet their obligations to care for their people? How do we wrestle with Philippians 4:19 where Paul said that God will meet all our needs if we will trust him?[5]

Missionaries commonly expect that the sponsoring church or mission agency will financially provide for them, but they find it difficult to ask for support when needed. Asian missionaries often think that to ask for money for their monthly support is the same as begging. They believe that if God has called them, he will provide. One missionary once said that she had no problem raising money for others but not for herself. It is much easier to speak for the needs of someone else than to tell the church of personal needs. It can be shameful in the Asian culture to ask for money for oneself, but it is an honor to help others raise their support.

Such cases and attitudes are pervasive. Another issue is how to develop mission work without becoming dependent on Western funds. To avoid this dependency, we have provided training in raising support. However, local churches and leaders must also be educated to understand the need to support missionaries (and their own pastors) at levels that allow for good member care.

Often the opposite is the case. Pastors and missionaries are supported at a minimal level, and they are expected to trust God to provide for their needs. In addition, some Asian missionaries are allowed to work in microenterprise projects while in ministry. Through these business projects, church planters may be able to earn some income that will help to supplement their monthly needs.

Such projects help to reduce both dependency on foreign support and the cultural shame of asking for support. Small loans have been provided for church-planting teams in order to help them start projects in their locations. Successful local projects can serve as testimonies to the community where they serve. Some of these small businesses are making Indian pickles, greeting cards, jam, tooth powder, and so on.

We believe that the sending churches and agencies need to take more responsibility for the financial support of their missionaries and also to creatively use whatever means available to keep the church planters in the field. To a large extent, this microenterprise process has not been accommodated in most Western missionary activity because it is thought to take time away from the real missionary activities.

Health Care Needs

Member care must be holistic in South Asia because there may be nothing set up for basic health care. We find it hard to convince our South Asian workers that they need to have insurance. It is not just the lack of finances that hinders the church planters from purchasing insurance. They must also overcome their negative attitudes about insurance companies. Five years ago an insurance plan for our church planters in South Asia was introduced. We received some quite discouraging, negative comments. Some of our workers said that they did not trust the insurance companies to actually pay compensation.

There is also a spiritual aspect to address. We heard one worker say that if he bought an insurance plan, it would indicate that he does not trust God. Is it unspiritual to enroll in an insurance plan? Some perceptual changes are needed for the missionaries to see health care resources, such as insurance, as important for their ministry effectiveness.

One organization in India partners with Missionary Upholders Trust (MUT) to provide basic medical care for their workers, should they need assistance. MUT will pay RS 15,000 (U.S. $325) of the medical expenses of the missionary if the worker is hospitalized. This may not sound like much from a Western point of view, but medical care in India is very inexpensive. They also provide for a minimal charge for a rest house in Vellore (South India) with twenty-two rooms to accommodate missionary families who are on medical-treatment leave.

This is very basic, and we need to look at other plans as well. However, even this level of care is difficult to achieve when a church does not provide this same level of coverage for its own pastors, or the church members themselves do not have access to health care. While the above is admirable, one shudders to think of the impact of the AIDS pandemic and of SARS, should they ever come into India.

Savings and Pension Programs

This is not a subject that is easily talked about in South Asia. Generally, the South Asians do not have the concept of savings, especially since the culture is philosophically fatalistic. People live from day to day and will only spend what they have. To approach the topic of savings is too foreign a concept, especially among those who are from the lower-income groups.

The majority of one mission's workers are from the villages or lower-income groups. They have not seen large amounts of money in their lives and have never been taught to save for their future needs. One of their church planters indicated that he is not able to set aside as little as RS 100 (U.S. $2.10) monthly toward savings, because all his income is needed to provide for his family. Our member care goal is to help these workers break out of this poverty mentality and believe that God may use new ways to meet their present and future needs.

This is not such a large issue for our expatriate workers because there is a strong state welfare program in the United Kingdom and

Social Security in the United States. In Asian countries there are no welfare states that can provide financial security once our missionaries retire. Therefore, it is even more crucial for the future of our church planters that we teach them the basic principles of savings.

Member Care Training Needs and Philosophy

As we continue to develop member care training needs, we have had to ask ourselves, Who is to be the primary member care provider in this context? In most cases, the answer is a coworker, not the specialized professional often held up as the ideal in the West. At best, there should be resource people close to the bases of ministry teams. Hopefully, small issues are handled as they arise so they do not escalate into difficult problems.

A training model needs to focus on who the caregivers and coaches are in missionary development. We start with *master care*, which means the information and growth we receive spiritually. This includes seeking the Lord's word and presence to help us with our burdens and weakness. Training programs need to start there and develop accessible strategies for applying spiritual truth in daily situations.

The next area is *self-care*, which means training member care workers how to care for themselves and to help missionaries take care of themselves. The next step is *one another care*. There are many things a team can do to help its members. The next point is *coach and pastoral care*. Many problems can be addressed with specific technical or pastoral assistance. Help with fundraising is an example of coaching care. *Clinical care* is the final step. Professionals are called in when there are issues that can't be properly addressed at any of the previous levels. In the best cases, people from all these levels operate all the time in the community of care surrounding the missionary.

In one sense, our innovative and forward-thinking strategies have been turned on their heads by our need to look backward, at least developmentally, in order to establish a firm foundation of member care. Member care in isolation, that is, when given to people without concern for the organizational and cultural milieu in which they live, witness, and work, can potentially isolate them from the local structures that can give them support.

In the West, member care occurs most frequently in this bifurcated and separated way. This is driven by a Western view of care occurring to an individual in a counseling environment and is involved with important professional issues, like confidentiality. However, a healthy organization takes care of its people in its own way, according to the cultural needs of its members. This is especially important from the perspective of the NSC agencies. We need to be sensitive to legal and professional issues, but we also need to call for commitment to biblical standards of care and concern and support for each other in an organizational context.

We are trying to help South Asian mission agencies lay a good foundation for basic support needs. These include financial, physical, medical, church-related, retirement-related needs, as well as emotional and psychological needs. We also want these agencies to take seriously the member care they can do themselves, without the external professional input. We believe a large number of issues can be effectively addressed in this way, keeping costs down in both money and people. As this foundation is being laid, we are helping organizations to address the need for professional care. However, we want this only in its proper time and place and not as the first line of support and care.

Some of the innovations we are helping to implement may prove to be strategic blessings. However, we hope that they will stimulate the NSC agencies in their own creative development, which will possibly take on completely new and different processes. As we look forward to the future of NSC ministry activities, we see plenty of concerns needing answers and creative applications of member care. These concerns include providing member care in places of perpetual violence and disorderliness, the increasing possibility of injury and martyrdom, the incessant open hostility of the receiving contexts, and the changing financial realities.

The old adage goes something like this: "Give a man a fish, and you feed him for a day. Teach a man to fish, and he can feed himself for the rest of his life." We are convinced that this may be no longer the case. Perhaps we have gotten too focused on the end result of catching fish. We may need to instead focus on more basic behaviors involved in the process of fishing, like key organizational concepts and strategies rather than equipment and technology. The results may not look like fishing at first, but these tactics may be just what the South Asian missionaries need to succeed in their kingdom work.

We believe that a synthesis of old and new information and technology that is adapted to local contexts and meets needs in a way that brings missionaries closer to the people they serve will be the pathway to greater outreach effectiveness. Member care, then, is not just about caring, but about effectively caring.

Brent Lindquist, PhD, is a licensed psychologist and president and CEO of Link Care Center, Fresno, California, a global counseling and consulting ministry. He is also a senior associate for marital health and member care for the Evangelical Fellowship of Mission Agencies. He consults with ministries worldwide on training and member care issues.

Ah Kie Lim is from peninsular Asia and has served Youth With A Mission (YWAM) in Asia for twenty-one years. For the last thirteen years, she has been the coordinator for member care development for the South Asia branch of YWAM, developing member care services and training programs. She has a master's degree in cross-cultural ministries and is studying for her PhD.

4
Innovation in Short-Term Mission

Roger Peterson

Should short-term mission be granted status as a new, *bona fide* missiological strategy? New it's not—but *bona fide*, and potentially strategic, it can be.

Yet before we ponder either the age or strategic possibilities of what Ralph Winter termed one of the "least anticipated major mutations in modern mission," let's first try to wrap our fingers around a definition. Short-term mission has always been set apart from career or long-term mission by the distinction of time. But how much time—two weeks? Two months? Two years? That's subjective and best determined on a case-by-case basis with a given sending entity and receiving field. A better definition would still encompass time but, rather than prescribing a fixed number of weeks or months or years, would use the term "temporary." A better definition would also add the terms "swift" and "volunteer" to more accurately describe what short-term mission really is.

Short-Term Mission Is Temporary

The on-field work of a short-term mission is temporary by design. Although long-term career mission can be cut short for various reasons, traditional long-term career missionaries tend to view their on-field contribution to be in primarily one location over the course of their lifetime. Short-termers view their on-field contribution as temporary, fully expecting to return home and reengage in whatever primary activity they left behind.

Career missionaries often buy the equivalent of a one-way ticket, because they're not sure when or if or how they'll return home. Short-term missionaries almost always buy round trip tickets, because they know exactly when they're coming home.

Temporary is not meant to suggest either good or bad. It is merely meant to help provide understanding of what short-term mission is and isn't and, therefore, how it can best be used as an innovative strategy when long-term career strategies are not a workable option.

Short-Term Mission Is Swift

Perhaps the greatest asset short-term mission brings to the table is its ability to swiftly place missionaries on-field. Traditional career missionaries often spend years in pre-field training. Short-termers can be deployed within just a few weeks or months—and some within just hours.

Certain types of work may require extended training for maximum effectiveness, such as Bible translation or frontier church planting within an unengaged, unreached people group. But many types of strategic mission work in certain fields do not require multiple years of preparation. In John 4:35 Jesus tells us that many fields are "ripe for harvest" right now and simply need laborers—now! Not theologians, not ripened missiologists, not seasoned thinkers—but laborers, people willing to sweat, work hard, and do whatever needs to be done. Remember, Jesus' only requirement for missionary service is empowerment of the Holy Spirit (Acts 1:8). Everything else—no matter how much sense it makes or how good it sounds—is human requirement.

When a field is crying for laborers, it sometimes takes years to form and send career missionary teams. Unfortunately, some career teams fall apart during their pre-field preparation, bonding, and deputation process. Worse yet, some crumble the first months on-field, producing virtually no kingdom return on the hundreds of thousands of dollars supporters invested in their intended efforts. But, in just a few months, short-termers can be recruited, trained, and sent. And there are times—many times—when the swift short-term strategy is actually the better financial strategy to employ.

Short-Term Mission Usually Consists of Volunteers

Most short-term missionaries are not paid a salary or wage. They are volunteers who donate their time. Long-term missionaries receive a salary—a fixed guarantee or raised monthly support. From the U.S. Internal Revenue Service's perspective, all long-term (paid) missionaries are either employees or subcontractors and are taxed accordingly. They're professionals—and not volunteers—by definition.

A paid professional also suggests a certain competence or expertise in the person's place of business. Because of extensive training, long-term missionaries are often screened and placed because of this expertise. On the other hand, short-termers often do not have the same extensive training and do not, therefore, have a professional level of competence with respect to comprehensive missiology. Therefore, it is usually correct to define short-term missionaries as nonprofessional volunteers.

Yes, short-term is also done by paid professionals. But, most of the time, short-term mission is done by nonpaid, nonprofessional volunteers.

How Long Has Short-Term Been Around?

Short-term mission strategies have been used as far back as the early biblical times. Moses used a short-term strategy at least twice. Consider the temporary, forty-day, twelve-man, fact-finding team he swiftly deployed from Kadesh into Canaan (Numbers 13–14). Also consider his temporary, five-day, two-man team swiftly deployed, with less than a day's notice, from Shittim to Jericho (Joshua 2). Samuel, Elijah, Elisha, Nehemiah, Jonah, Jesus, the apostle Paul, Philip, Barnabas, Peter, Tychicus, Titus, Apollos, the women, the twelve disciples, and the seventy (seventy-two) disciples were also involved in short-term mission strategies that were all temporary, swift, and usually done in a nonprofessional, volunteer context. How long has short-term mission been around? More than three thousand years.

What Are the Current Short-Term Mission Trends?

With an eye toward bona fide, strategic use of short-term mission for world evangelization, practitioners need to note the following several trends affecting the bigger short-term mission picture: exponential growth, codified standards, agencies no longer being the only sending entity, and improved literature.

Exponential Growth

In 1965 student researcher Thomas Chandler noted only 540 individuals from North America involved in short-term mission. In 1989 an estimate by a Fuller School of World Mission doctoral student put the number at 120,000. Three years later it had more than doubled to 250,000. By 1998 Evangelical Fellowship of Mission Agencies (EFMA) vice president and former InterVarsity Mission Urbana director John Kyle had research that put the figure at 450,000. In 2003 Peterson, Aeschliman, and Sneed estimated at least 1 million short-termers were being sent out from a globally-sent perspective each year. In 2004 Robert Priest, director of the doctoral program in Intercultural Studies at Trinity Evangelical Divinity School, reported that he was beginning to locate data suggesting the number could be as high as *4 million*.

Who is sending all these short-termers? In the United States alone, there are currently at least 40,000 sending entities (35,000 churches, 3,700 agencies, and more than 1,000 schools) that do the sending.

Why the explosion of growth? Among the myriad of possible answers lie the following plausible explanations spanning the past six decades—all of which are sociologically immense and, therefore, outside of any missiological ability to direct or control:

1940s: World War II. Many mission societies began soon after the war ended. There was a flood of energetic, enthusiastic young people coming home from the war. Many had traveled far and wide, seeing devastation in much of the world first hand. For the first time in history, we saw relatively young people who had experience in world-wide travel and who had a global perspective. Combine that with a passion for God's glory among the lost, and it's easy to see why direct hands-on involvement in Christian mission began growing after the war.

1950s: Modern Airplane Travel. The idea of the average citizen flying commercially didn't really take hold until a decade after the war. By the mid-1950s more planes were in the air; air travel was not seen as the exclusive domain of the rich or the military; and, the cost of a flight was within the financial reach of more citizens. As a direct result, average Western Christians could virtually go anywhere in the world with relative ease and speed.

1960s: The Peace Corps. U.S. President John Kennedy launched the Peace Corps in 1961. By 2005 more than 182,000 North Americans had become Peace Corps volunteers in 138 nations. This was a government-sanctioned "blessing" to travel abroad and volunteer time making a difference in a developing country for a cause greater than one's self. Did this have a positive impact on the growth of Christian short-term missions? I think it's safe to assume that it did.

1960s–1990s: The Rise of Postmodernity. Thanks in part to the growing societal distrust of leaders in the 1960s (due largely to the confusion and manipulation surrounding such megaevents as the Kennedy assassination and the Vietnam War), young people began fighting stock answers and prodding behind what they were beginning to perceive as leadership rhetoric and spin. They began demanding that experience and action match what was said. Experience, therefore, was being equated with truth. The experience-equals-truth equation (which was becoming one of the characteristic hallmarks of emergent postmodern thinking) was further accelerated by the mesmerizing sight-sound-sensory experience being generated by the film, television, and music industries. The impact of these two sociological phenomena on current postmodern Christianity is that it compels its pew-sitting participants into the actual hands-on experience of missions.

1990–2000s: The Internet and World Wide Web. Contact with faraway places is no longer the domain of the news media or the highly networked socialite. Average people now easily communicate with missionaries in faraway places, making the world seem a much smaller place. As my writing colleague Wayne Sneed notes, "Before the Internet, Joe the missionary was someone we heard about from the pulpit on Sunday nights. Now, going five thousand miles to help Joe my friend (who e-mails me every week) is revolutionizing Christian mission."

The Holy Spirit. Rapidly growing numbers alone don't prove God is behind the flurry of short-term mission growth. Yet the Lord of the Harvest cries out to us to pray for laborers and commands us to go and make disciples. And two thousand years later, with somewhere around 4.8 billion people currently crawling their way along the wide road to hell, only an insane person would refuse to recognize the church's colossal failure. But because short-term mission allows swift, immediate response by any believer to the action explicitly demanded by the gospel; because short-term allows temporary engagement by Christian people not called, or not yet called, into full-time professional ministry (realistically, that's the overwhelming majority of the church); and because short-term mission allows lay volunteers (again, that's the overwhelming majority of the church) opportunity to perform what God commands of all disciples—regardless of age, gender, race, culture, training, social status, economic status, or experience—perhaps, short-term mission is a current tool the Holy Spirit has launched in order to accelerate completion of the Father's command.

Codified Standards

The missiological validity of short-term mission has been rightly questioned on countless occasions, especially when it pertains to frontier mission work among unengaged and unreached peoples. The anecdotal evidence abounds on both sides of the fence: there are stories of scandal and selfishness; there are stories of success and indelibly changed lives. But until recently, no "standards," no "best practices" have existed to help mission strategists separate the short-term wheat from the short-term chaff.

Developed over the course of two years by more than four hundred people from across the United States, the "U.S. Standards of Excellence in Short-Term Mission" (SOE) was launched in October 2003 (www.STMstandards.org). It formalizes the ethical and operating procedures many sending entities believe should be standardized. The SOE helps improve any short-term mission program by mandating periodic training and peer review for sending-entity leaders. For the first time in U.S. history, a national code of ethics now exists to help donors, parents, volunteers, churches, field personnel, and others distinguish effective short-term mission programs from glorified vacations.

Agencies No Longer Being the Only Sending Entity

The number of short-term mission sending agencies is on the rise (around 3,700 U.S. agencies currently send short-term missionaries). Many of these groups are small "mom and pop" operations that know nothing of the EFMA or IFMA (Interdenominational Foreign Mission Association) or similar traditional mission networks. But what they do know is that God called them to send as many short-term groups as they can muster to help a certain people in a certain country somewhere in the world.

However, these 3,700 agencies pale in comparison to the 35,000 U.S. churches that do the same. Thousands of people in thousands of churches also believe that God has called them to send their own church teams to help certain people in certain countries somewhere in the world. Increasingly, the church sees itself as the direct recipient of the Great Commission and is beginning to put its local feet to the worldwide task.

Christian schools (colleges, universities, high schools, and home schools) are also hearing the Great Commission call and responding personally. Schools now send thousands of short-termers, often issuing academic credit for the effort. Some of the major school-sending entities include Wheaton College, Master's College, Bethany College of Missions, Azusa Pacific University, Messiah College, Vanguard University, John Brown University, Northwestern College (Iowa), Northwestern College (Minnesota), Bethel University, Trinity

International University, Biola University, Taylor University, Point Loma College, Gordon College, Oral Roberts University, and others.

Other Christian institutions—none of them chartered or organized for Christian mission—are also beginning to respond personally to the Great Commission. Christian radio stations, campus fellowships, community hospitals, and other groups have founding documents that state the purpose of the given group, and the purpose is something *other* than cross-cultural Christian mission. Yet these groups too are beginning to send short-term missionaries.

Improved Literature

Until recently, little solid literature existed to guide short-term mission practitioners in their work. The little that was available was often self-published and usually provided only anecdotal evidence to support the bias (either for or against) of the given author. Or, it was a graduate study so entrenched in the given school's academic requirements that the average practitioner couldn't make use of it (nor could the average practitioner easily get a copy of the study in the first place).

Fortunately, we are now entering a season in the short-term mission industry where better editors and known publishers are beginning to release quality books and other material authored with solid content that is directly applicable to the short-term practitioner's needs.

What Is the Future of Short-Term Mission?

Should the Lord tarry, the next few years will likely challenge the mission community at-large to grapple with these three changes: (1) fields will limit their short-terms to proven groups; (2) schools will offer formal, for-credit academic training in short-term mission methods; and (3) new short-term mission networks will bypass traditional networks in attendance and membership numbers.

Fields Will Limit Their Short-Terms to Proven Groups

Receiving mission fields will begin to recognize the value of short-term groups submitting to the U.K. Code of Best Practice, or the Canadian Code of Best Practice, or the U.S. Standards of Excellence in Short-Term Mission. As a result, many fields will begin limiting the short-term missionaries they receive to only those who comply with one of these code-setting networks. Receiving fields will, therefore, have demanded—and can now enforce—a higher quality of short-term mission.

Schools Will Offer Formal, For-Credit Academic Training in Short-Term Mission Methods

Several Christian schools now provide courses in world missions, and many of those provide entire degree programs in some aspect of missiology or Christian cross-cultural study as well. But, as of this writing, I know of no credit-granting institution that provides an entire, for-credit degree program in short-term mission.

But some savvy school administrator somewhere will soon recognize not only the importance of providing for-credit courses but also an entire degree program in effective short-term mission methods and strategies. The first school to actually figure this out will have applicants lined up a mile long waiting to get in.

New Short-Term Mission Networks Will Bypass Traditional Networks in Attendance and Membership Numbers

Traditional mission networks such as the IFMA and the EFMA—as good and necessary as they are—have reached plateaus and now struggle to maintain membership of over one hundred mission agencies each. Unless such groups are able to retool their understanding of who the new mission-sending entities are, the overwhelming majority of the forty thousand U.S.-based short-term sending entities won't give them a second thought.

Short-term sending entities are already beginning to band together, completely bypassing the traditional mission networks. The U.K. Code of Best Practice is less than ten years old and already has more than two hundred members. The U.S. Standards of Excellence in Short-Term Mission is just two years old (as of this writing) and already has eighty members. It is forecasting membership of more than eight hundred sending entities within the next five years. The National Short-Term Mission Conference (held every January in either California or Florida) draws around three hundred attendees each year, helping to train short-term-mission team leaders and improve short-term-mission programs.

Older conferences and associations must make radical changes in order to incorporate the newer, short-term practitioners into their much-needed spheres of influence. Older conferences and associations have an immense wealth of experience and insight to draw from—all of which is desperately needed by short-term mission practitioners. But history shows an overwhelming refusal of many such older groups to adequately adjust to the changing times. And the result will be newer short-term-mission networks that spring up and completely bypass the very groups that could—and should—be helping them.

Conclusion

Short-term mission has been around for a long, long time—at least three thousand years. It has been sometimes composed of sloppy work and selfish agendas. But with or without the help of the older, traditional-mission networks, the pressure of forty thousand U.S. short-term sending entities and their one million or more short-termers has already created its own standards of best practice, better training, and launched networks designed to improve the effectiveness of short-term-mission efforts.

Short-term mission can be a *bona fide* and, perhaps, the best missiological strategy when the field need is for *swift, temporary,* non-professional *volunteers*.

Case Study #1: A School
Bethany College of Missions (BCOM),
Bloomington, Minnesota

Although recently amended to a much more intensive short-term phase, a core piece of the original four-year-curriculum requirements of Bethany College of Mission was short-term mission. Not short-term mission *trips*. But short-term mission *outreaches*. Not just one—but two of them prior to graduation.

Between their freshman and sophomore years, all students were sent out in teams of six to twelve students per team on three-week outreaches around the globe, including many fields where Bethany's career missionaries work. Students didn't waste time just observing missionaries or national people but engaged hands-on in the work being done by the receiving missionaries and their national hosts. Many of the college faculty were trained to lead these teams. Returning for their sophomore year, students (and the faculty who accompanied them) continued their study of mission and the Bible no longer from a theoretical vacuum but from the womb of actual, hands-on missionary experience—student and teacher together.

One year later, students then spent their entire junior year (nine months) overseas on a second short-term outreach, usually in pairs or much smaller teams. Students tackled the local language, wrestled with the culture, survived its gastrointestinal consequences, and at times even battled the ideologies of missiology with the local missionaries. All the while, students remained engaged in hands-on missionary work as determined by their field-receiving hosts. Some students had a great nine-month outreach while others crashed and burned. After students returned for their senior year, the faculty spent the remaining year applying balm to students' battle scars and working through all the issues encountered while on the field.

When students graduated that fourth year, most were ready for some serious kingdom work wherever God sent them in the world.

Case Study #2: A Mission Agency Youth With A Mission (YWAM), Worldwide

Loren Cunningham launched YWAM in 1960 as an evangelistic outreach program focused on getting youth into short-term mission. Now forty-five years later, YWAM's website lists nearly sixteen thousand full-time staff members and more than twenty-five thousand short-termers in more than 150 nations. Yet when speaking off the record with some YWAM leaders, unofficial estimates run as high as 300 thousand or more short-termers per year. YWAM is unquestionably the largest mission-sending group in the world, not because of their financial fundraising savvy and ability to pay high-buck salaries but because of their innovative use of short-term missionaries.

In their early years, YWAM's growth didn't really take off until they initiated the Discipleship Training School (DTS). Although it varies from one YWAM base to another, the usual three-month DTS consists of about two months of training while living in community (students and staff together) followed by a one-month, short-term mission outreach, with everyone trusting the Lord to provide all the financial support needed. DTS focuses on knowing God and then on making him known, using an extremely high level of personal student-teacher interaction involving key teaching topics that result in personal-issues resolution and much prayer. DTS students are taught to hear the voice of God and then obey.

What makes YWAM unique is that it is the only missionary organization that has had ministry outreach within *every single geopolitical nation in the world*. No other missionary society has come remotely close to accomplishing this. But YWAM has, because they've come up with a relatively simple short-term-mission system to *swiftly* and *temporarily* send *volunteers* to every corner of the globe.

Case Study #3: A Church
Perimeter Church, Atlanta, Georgia

Perimeter Church (3,500 members; 5,000 weekly worshipers) began in 1977. Perimeter held its first mission conference in 1979 and sent its first short-termer (one person for two years) to Sudan in 1982 and their first short-term team in 1986. Fast forward to 2004, where Perimeter now trains a cadre of church volunteers who in turn train, prepare, and debrief the dozens of "GO (Global Outreach) Journey" short-term teams the church sends out each year.

The innovative factor in Perimeter's use of short-term teams is that they work primarily within the 10-40 Window, including many restricted-access nations. Each of Perimeter's GO Journey teams works with one of Perimeter's national church-planting partners, specifically assisting their long-term church-planting efforts. And throughout the pre-field, on-field, and into the post-field portions of each short-term outreach, Perimeter leaders are also intentional about helping develop Christian attitudes and life-change behaviors in each of their short-termers.

Perimeter's short-term teams work well in the "mission frontiers" of this challenging part of the world, because Perimeter has invested (and still continues to reinvest) time and money with their national church-planting partners in order to make it work for everyone involved—the senders, the goers, and the receivers.

Innovation in Short-Term Mission

Case Study #4: A Church
Southeast Christian Church, Louisville, Kentucky

SECC began in 1965, growing in less than forty years to more than seventeen thousand weekly worshipers. SECC's first short-term mission was a large team of sixty people (too big, says Global Missions minister Brian Wright) to Jamaica in 1990. In 2002, SECC sent fifty-seven short-term teams—more than seven hundred and fifty SECC members—to twenty nations.

What makes SECC's short-term mission outreaches innovative and effective are two items: their strategic and accountable link to the field; and their three-level "line upon line, precept upon precept" methodologies. SECC's "Great Adventure" mission outreaches go only to SECC-supported partners (strategic link to the field) and are planned within three levels: (1) Exploration (closer, easier, less costly, about five days); (2) Excursion (outside the United States, more cross-culture, about ten days); and (3) Expedition (culturally and geographically far away, two weeks or longer).

Case Study #5: A Radio Station
KTIS AM / FM, St Paul, Minnesota

Started in 1949 when Billy Graham was president of Northwestern College in St. Paul, Minnesota, KTIS has grown to more than 250 thousand weekly listeners in the central Minnesota and western Wisconsin area. Additionally, their SkyLight Network now feeds programming to more than two hundred and fifty Christian media affiliates across the United States. KTIS currently places in the top five of one of the highly competitive "morning drive" Twin Cities markets, which consists of dozens of well-financed secular stations.

In the late 1990s, Music and Promotions director Dan Wynia wound up in Belize for a few days and came back to the station with an unquenchable burden to help ramp up evangelistic broadcast efforts in Belize. KTIS has since provided money, equipment, and technical expertise on several occasions—most of that delivered through short-term efforts. More recently (2003 and 2004), KTIS partnered with my organization, STEM Ministries. After selecting six of their own people, we recruited on-air another two dozen people to form a team of thirty short-term missionaries (more than seventy listeners made preliminary application for this team). These "average listeners" were trained, and joined the KTIS staff to provide a three-day media seminar for Christian broadcasters in Belize, some on-site technical trouble shooting, prayer-walking for the peoples of Belize, some construction and building efforts, and ministry to HIV-infected prisoners.

KTIS discovered an innovative way to put international feet to the gospel they broadcast locally every day. They discovered how to help transform passive listeners into active missionaries. Their secret? Short-term mission.

ROGER PETERSON is CEO of STEM Int'l (Short-Term Evangelical Missions: STEM Ministries, STEM Share, STEM Training, STEM Press). He chairs the Fellowship of Short-Term Mission Leaders and the U.S. Standards of Excellence in Short-Term Mission. He publishes *Mission Maker Magazine* and is the lead co-author of *Maximum Impact Short-Term Mission*.

5
Innovation in Training Writers and Publishers
John Maust

Knowing about my interest in Latin America, the late Kenneth Kantzer, then editor of *Christianity Today* magazine, posed this intriguing question: "Why don't you go to Latin America on a short leave of absence? You can work on your Spanish, and when you come back you'll be able to translate articles by Latin correspondents for the magazine."

Other mission-minded staff at the magazine—men like Jim Reapsome and Harry Genet—encouraged the idea. So in the early 1980s I took a three-month leave from my job in the news department at *Christianity Today* and went to Costa Rica to study Spanish. Little did I suspect where that three-month trip would ultimately lead.

God gave me a love for Latin America, and, ultimately, I wound up leaving the magazine (friends considered this crazy) to explore full-time ministry possibilities in the region. During an extended trip around Central and South America, staying mostly in youth hostels and traveling on buses, I asked missionaries and Latin pastors how a North American journalist like me could fit into Christian work there. "We need more Latin-authored Christian books and articles," they invariably said. "You can come and train Latin Christians to write."

To my disbelief, they said from 80 to 90 percent of all Christian books in Spanish had been translated from English or another language. It didn't make sense. Why would Latin Americans want to read a Christian book about time management or youth ministry, for example, written by authors from a country with cultural, economic, and family values so different from their own?

I would spend four years in Peru as a missionary journalist with a primary focus on writer training. Later I got involved full-time in a ministry of equipping and encouraging local Christian publishers and authors, primarily in the developing world, through an organization called Media Associates International.

Everywhere in my travels today, I meet Christian men and women with incredible stories and a passion to write and get published. But many of their stories remain untold. The striking imbalance of Western translations remains. In some parts of the world, at least four in every five Christian books has been translated from English or originally written in a culture foreign to the reader. One of the most strategic ministries today is getting local Christian writers published in the hard places of the world.

Strengthening the Church

The church in every country and culture needs skilled Christian writers who can speak to the unique interests and needs of its people. Author Tim Stafford has rightly said the strength of a nation's church lies in direct proportion to its body of locally authored and produced Christian literature. Yet the preponderance of translations and imported books props up the false notion that Christianity is purely a Western or imported religion and thus irrelevant, if not repugnant (depending on one's view of Western culture).

In a provocative address, "Reclaiming the Great Conversation," to international Christian publishers at the 2002 Frankfurt Book Fair, Mark Carpenter said, "The long-term effects... have yet to be weighed, but I am convinced that one of the end results is the ultimate reinforcement of the notion that modern Christianity is essentially U.S.-based and, therefore, foreign to the local context.

"I remember a young Brazilian Christian psychologist who vehemently disagreed with a North American author's instruction about raising children. It took her awhile to sort out what was biblical and what was merely cultural. As Brazilian Christians read our countless translated books, my concern is that some may end up thinking of evangelical Christianity as patently foreign, nice but not vital, interesting but not indispensable, commendable but not relevant. Don't get me wrong. These readers do need to be exposed to North America's best and most engaging writers, but a steady diet of nothing but foreign literature will not nourish or sustain them."

What the West Needs to Hear

Not only is indigenous Christian literature important for the maturation of the national church, we in the West need to hear the stories and experiences of fellow believers in the developing world—stories that will inspire or perhaps jolt us from our spiritual lethargy.

"By 2005," Philip Jenkins wrote in an article in *The Atlantic Monthly*, "50 percent of the Christian population will be in Africa and Latin America, and another 17 percent will be in Asia. Those proportions will grow steadily."[1] The strength of the church is moving South, said Jenkins. Ironically, publication of local authors is least active in those parts of the world where the church is growing fastest.

In my contacts with Christian writers around the world, I frequently meet men and women who professed faith as a result of reading translated books like those of C.S. Lewis or Josh McDowell. But why aren't readers in the West growing in their faith or even coming to Christ through reading the translated works of Christian authors from Colombia, Côte d'Ivoire, or Cambodia?

The Development of Christian Writers

By encouraging the development of local Christian writers and disseminating their work abroad, both the national and global community of believers is strengthened. For writer development to be effective, at least four key elements must be in place: (1) involvement by a local publisher; (2) an active, caring editor; (3) ongoing encouragement; and (4) financial and other recognition to the author.

Involvement by a Local Publisher

When I first got involved in writer training in Peru, I was traveling around the country trying to find and encourage Christians in the ministry of writing. Colleagues and I managed to stimulate some interest in writing. (I remember one eager writer living in cramped quarters with a big family, so her only space to write was the emergency ward lobby of a nearby hospital.) We provided some practical teaching and tools for getting the job done. But as writers began to produce quality manuscripts, we realized something: Where would these writers get published?

At the time Peru had no local Protestant publishing house. Neither was there an interdenominational Christian magazine. Writers had only a few newsletters and denominational publications from which to choose. We risked fanning into flame a passion for writing, only to see it doused by the discouragement of nowhere to get published.

Innovation in Training Writers and Publishers

Colleagues and I wound up starting a couple of small newsletters to provide writers an outlet. We also encouraged the more advanced writers to submit their work to publishers in other Latin American nations or to local newspapers and secular media. Some churches also had "mural newspapers," bulletin boards where members could post articles outside the church door.

This experience taught me a valuable lesson: Writer training that is not linked with an existing publishing structure will likely prove futile, and it will certainly be frustrating to the writers. Whenever possible, author training should be conducted with the full participation, if not sponsorship, of a local publisher or group of publishers.

Therefore, publisher development is just as vital as author development. Often publishing houses are started by visionaries with no business experience. Veteran international publisher Peter Cunliffe often says, "Christian publishing is 100 percent business and 100 percent ministry." If a publisher is not financially viable, there will be no publishing ministry. Peter travels the world as a kind of "apostle to publishers" in the developing world, giving on-site guidance and mentoring on such things as writing a business plan, preparing book budgets, and cash-flow statements.

Many Christian publishers in Africa, Asia, and Latin America face a constant lack of capital for the editorial development of new titles, reprinting of popular backlist titles, and marketing. Compounding the problem is the extremely low purchasing power in countries where disposable income for books is scarce. Western publishers could provide targeted grants for publishing capital or consider annual tithes either to some selected Christian publishers or to a publisher-training program. However, I would couple any financial investment in an indigenous publisher with hands-on training and interaction on topics as basic as developing business plans.

Fortunately, some Western publishers are contributing funds or other resources to agencies and groups involved in training overseas publishers, and they are making staff available to serve as trainers.

Key Role of the Editor

A skilled editor makes the best writer trainer. Too often, start-up publishers view the editor as someone who corrects spelling and grammar goofs—nothing more. Copyediting and proofreading are part of the job in the small, one-editor publishing operation. But the effective editor develops ideas for books and articles that fulfill the publisher's vision and then goes out and finds the writer who will write those manuscripts.

Much like a loving midwife, the editor helps the author successfully give birth to the manuscript. There may be some pain involved in the editorial process, as in childbirth, but joy over the long-awaited "baby" quickly banishes any memory of earlier discomfort.

"Editors can't teach talent," widely respected editor Judith Markham writes in *Servanthood and the Christian Editor*.[2] "We can only teach writers to be more serious about their own talent and encourage them to develop it better. Part of the editor's service is to bring out the best in the writer.

"Writers are fragile people. They may be tough as old boots on the outside, but inside they can be a complicated mixture of insecurity and authority, pride and humility. Editors must understand this and learn how to deal with it appropriately. We must learn to read between the lines—to discover exactly what form of encouragement a writer needs."

A skilled editor helps the writer develop a well-conceived theme on which to construct the book or article. Also, the editor keeps the author's focus on the intended reader. In conversations with editors overseas, I encourage them to seek authors from all walks of life, not just the theologians, but schoolteachers, doctors, and housewives. (I think of Delfino, a Mexican truck driver, who wrote eloquent poetry in his down times at work.)

Encouragement in Season

Writers in the developing world work largely alone and without interaction with like-minded peers. A bit of encouragement may be the determining factor in whether an aspiring writer quits or perseveres. Linking an experienced writer with a beginner is helpful in this regard.

An East African writer at one of the biennial LITT-WORLD conferences organized by Media Associates International told me that she and a writer from Trinidad worked up their nerve to request a meeting with two well-known authors from the United States who were attending the same conference.

"We sought them out to hear firsthand their experiences," the African writer said. "How did they know they had a calling to be writers? How could we tell whether we were harboring delusions of grandeur? How did they keep writing when there was no more write left in them? From where did they draw their inspiration?

"I remember coming away from that dinner table feeling invigorated and just about ready to take on the world, pen in hand. It wasn't that they had all the answers but, rather, that they had been where we were and understood implicitly where we were coming from."

Any editor or trainer should also remind aspiring authors that writing is, indeed, a ministry. Christian leaders are in short supply in many countries. That a gifted preacher or teacher would spend hours alone writing may seem inconceivable to friends and family who may plead, "We *need* you with us!" So even the best writers like Patricia Vergara of Peru begin to question their motivations and priorities.

In the book *La Aventura de Escribir*, Patricia described a transformational moment for her in this regard.[3] During a seminary course she attended on leadership training, Patricia found herself deeply moved as the professor prayed that every student would discover God's unique purpose for his or her life.

Heavily involved at the megachurch pastored by her husband, Patricia sensed the Holy Spirit telling her to give priority to her writing and give up some of the other things she was doing. "I began to think about the church and my responsibilities there," she recalled. "The faces of the different people who needed me and put demands on my time started going through my mind. I wept and wept, because I realized that I would need to make some really big adjustments and changes in my life to fulfill my calling."

When the professor gave the class a five-minute break, Patricia ran to the women's room to dry her tears. On the way she met one of the school secretaries who handed her a note that had just arrived by e-mail. Patricia thought this strange, considering she never received e-mail letters at the seminary.

"That letter moved me even more deeply," she recalled. "It came from a Chilean woman, also a pastor's wife. She didn't know me personally, but she had read my book, *Yo No Pedi Ser Oro* (*I Didn't Ask to Be Made Gold*). In tender and beautiful words, she told me how the book had ministered to her. She asked me to continue writing, and she said she prayed continually for me. This was a beautiful confirmation from God . . . I longed to give him my will, my talent, even my ministry and responsibilities so that I could fulfill his purpose for me."

For writers in the developing world, otherwise routine tasks just take longer—lines at public offices and stores, mind-numbing traffic snarls, and frequent power blackouts. And imagine starting a serious writing ministry in a place wracked by violence, war, or political turmoil.

Bakanoba Kivy traveled from war-ravaged eastern Congo to a Christian writers' workshop in Kenya. On the last morning of the workshop, Kivy flashed a big, but bleary-eyed, smile. "I was up all last night," he told me. "Because of the violence back home, I knew that if I waited until I returned home to start the novel, it would never happen." (At this time Kivy and his family were living as refugees in Uganda after barely escaping the tribal bloodshed with their lives.) Giving encouragement—not just for writing but of a personal or even spiritual nature—is just as important, if not more so, than teaching writing technique.

Author Payment and Recognition

Some publishers will pay the printer or graphic designer without hesitation, but the author is not part of the equation. As trainers, we have a responsibility both to encourage aspiring Christian writers and to encourage their payment for published work.

Fledgling publishers in some countries are known to ask authors to pay *them* for publishing their books. This is not a criticism of overseas publishers, but reflects the need for an ongoing, awareness-raising process that authors need to be recognized (and eat) too. At a recent training seminar in South America, an author showed me a well-written manuscript in which a local publisher had expressed interest. I congratulated her on this accomplishment. But then she lowered her voice and asked me in confidence, "What do you think I should do? The publisher would like to publish my book, but they say I need to pay half of the printing cost. I don't have that kind of money."

Author payment can take the form of a flat amount upon completion of an acceptable manuscript. Or, it could be an advance, along with a royalty based on sales of the book. Even in the most financially strapped cases, the publisher can provide the author a certain number of free copies of the book or publication, or invite the author to a special meal, or otherwise recognize the author's work in a way that makes the author feel part of the team.

Another form of investment in writers is author-assistance funds. Lawrence, an African writer and editor, recently told a long-time acquaintance, "I have three novels in my mind. I can actually see the words on the printed page. But I just can't get the books written."

Eager to help Lawrence realize his dream, the friend probed to learn what was blocking Lawrence's writing output. It turned out that finances were an issue. With some additional funds, Lawrence could hire some freelance help at the magazine that would release him for personal writing. Also, funds would enable Lawrence to get away for occasional two-week writing retreats where he could focus solely on writing.

Soon after his meeting with Lawrence, the friend contacted some colleagues and between them they raised a modest author-assistance grant for Lawrence. The gift proved liberating to Lawrence and jump-started his work on the three novels.

One final note related to finances: The well-intentioned flood of give-away and heavily subsidized Christian books from the West can undercut and weaken the publishing efforts of fledgling local publishers in the developing world. Local publishers and booksellers will tell you one of their biggest headaches is customers complaining about having to pay a fair price for locally produced books. "Christian literature should be free," people say, hearkening to the past history of free Christian books and literature.

Some Training Formats That Work

One or a combination of training formats can yield results in local author development. These include:

- **Writer workshops.** These need the involvement of a local Christian publishing group, when possible. Participants should be carefully selected. Don't fill the time with teaching; allow at least 40 percent of workshop time to actual writing, with hands-on critique by facilitators.

Innovation in Training Writers and Publishers

- **Internships.** Internships with editors or publishers are best suited for more advanced writers, who can take full advantage and enhance talent and ability already there.

- **Tutorials.** One-to-one tutorials are extremely effective, but also the most time consuming. Experienced Western writers could partner with overseas colleagues in a mentoring role, both face-to-face and through e-mail. Don't rely solely on online training: "In Asia, we need to see faces," a publisher in the Philippines said.

- **Writing retreats.** Writing retreats, held far from participants' churches and other duties, facilitate extended writing time without distractions. Consider using evenings for read-aloud sessions.

- **Joint authorship.** Certain InterVarsity-related groups and other publishers have used this technique effectively. A group of writers is invited to each write a chapter on a different facet of the same book topic. Daniel Bourdanné, general secretary of the International Fellowship of Evangelical Students, London, when he was head of the IFES-related movements in Francophone Africa, invited a hand-picked group of writers to each contribute a chapter for a book on tribalism, a problem causing bloodshed and strife across the continent.

- **Magazine projects.** Magazines and newsletters are an excellent training ground for future authors. Participating writers learn to meet deadlines and work with an editor, plus they get the satisfaction of seeing their work in print. In the 1980s Tim Stafford launched the successful *Step*, a youth magazine in Kenya, on the strength of local writers that he trained.

- **Writers' groups.** A successful writers' group needs an organized leader able to keep participants involved and interested, with each meeting having a specific focus. The Christian writer's fellowship in the Philippines has thrived for more than fifteen years. We know the kinds of books that emerged from

"The Inklings" (an informal group of writers including J.R.R. Tolkien and C.S. Lewis). Couldn't the same thing happen today in other parts of the world?

- **Awareness-raising seminars.** Consider holding a "Day of the Christian Author" in local Christian schools and groups. To harvest the next generation of Christian writers, we need to start watering and cultivating early.

- **Contests.** Contests are a good way of "casting out the net," trying to find skilled and potential Christian writers lurking under the surface.

- **Product-driven training.** Conduct training with a specific product in mind. For instance, Christian magazine editor Elisabeth Isais in Mexico organized a short-story workshop. She raised funds to cover the printing of a short-story anthology composed of the best stories from the workshop. Participants' motivation and output visibly increased after Elisabeth told participants they would be published in the anthology if they completed a quality manuscript. Indeed, the book got published, and the one thousand copies quickly sold out.

- **Seminaries and Bible colleges.** Church leaders and pastors consistently prepare material for teaching and preaching. Why not help them communicate effectively in writing and, thereby, multiply their present ministries? Surprisingly, few seminaries and Bible colleges offer classes in writing for publication.

Results are best measured over time. So trainers should not get discouraged if published authors don't emerge after a short workshop. (Imagine holding a week-long soccer workshop for beginners and then expecting them to compete at a World Cup level.) Not every writer we encourage will persevere. But some will, and therein lies the hope and challenge.

Recently, I received a letter from Fernando Mosquera, a seminary professor in Colombia, who attended a writing workshop ten years ear-

Innovation in Training Writers and Publishers

lier. He said he had published two books—commentaries on Habakkuk and Ephesians. Another book had been accepted by a major publisher.

"As you see," Fernando wrote, "the workshop in Medellín yielded excellent results. I want to thank you for helping me discover my writing talent and for having taught me in the workshop. Every time people read my books, they will receive the impact of [your] ministry."

Signs of Progress

Other published writers like Fernando are emerging in Latin America, Asia, Africa, and Eastern Europe. Progress is being made. For example, when I first went to Peru twenty years ago, there were no Christian publishers; today there are three. Also, the many grassroots Christian publishers in Latin America have formed a network, *Letra Viva*, which is giving invaluable help to its member agencies in distribution, training, marketing, and joint representation at book fairs.

In Eastern Europe numerous magazine and book publishers sprang up after the fall of communism, and previously silenced writers began to surface. Sharon Mumper's Magazine Training Institute has provided training to scores of staff from Christian magazines in Eastern Europe and the former Soviet Union.

One magazine success story in East Europe is *Inspiracje*, a full-color publication for general readers giving a Christian perspective on popular topics such as family, physical and emotional health, movies, books, and culture. The magazine founders, Henryk and Alina Wieja, are cultivating a cadre of skilled local writers who speak Christianly to matters of importance to the Polish people. (Alina launched the magazine after sensing God speaking to her through a reading of Habakkuk 2:2: "Write down the revelation and make it plain on tablets so that a herald may run with it.")

Henryk and Alina also began writing books. With some trepidation, they recently approached a major secular book distributor and asked if he would carry Henryk's latest book. The company executive immediately accepted the book and astonished the Wiejas by asking, "Do you have any more books like this one? I'll take all that you have."

In the early 1990s, Besa Shapllo started *Miracle* magazine for grade-school children in Albania, previously the Soviet bloc's most atheistic state. Her magazine quickly attracted an intensely loyal following. "Miracle Clubs," composed of child readers, formed around the country, and the government's education ministry allowed distribution of the magazine in the public schools. A girl once asked Besa if there were plans to launch another magazine for older children. Besa said not yet. The girl sadly shook her head. "If getting older means I can no longer read *Miracle* magazine, then I don't want to grow up."

Power of the Written Word

Some people, like veteran editor Babu Verghese of India, believe the ministry role of print media will increase, not decrease, in the years ahead. "Literature is the future of Indian evangelism," said Babu. "The era of public Christian crusades, conventions, and open-air preaching is over in India. Witnessing has to be done very discreetly through friendship evangelism and passing on effective literature. Therefore, we need trained writers and editors who can address relevant issues. The need is urgent as the door for evangelism is being closed at a fast pace."

As an evangelistic or pre-evangelistic medium, print is especially effective. "In some respects, print has the potential to penetrate resistance and defenses better than any other medium," notes author Tim Stafford. "Print is portable. You can take most literature anywhere you want. This enables print to penetrate places where other communications media cannot.

"Print is also silent and, therefore, potentially very private. People can read something and no one in their family may know they are doing it. They can find a private space, free from pressure, to consider a thought. So, print has the ability to speak to that person very inoffensively.... Print has a powerful way of breaking down defenses."

What I find exciting is that writers in the developing world are going into the marketplace of ideas and not limiting their message to the small Christian subculture. At a writer workshop organized by Besa Shapllo in Albania, a long banner spread across the front of the meeting room. "Without spiritual renewal, our country cannot be transformed," it said. The writers had come because they intended to transform Albanian society through the written word.

To remind me of this same challenge, I keep the yellowing registration form of a Peruvian student at one of my workshops twenty years ago. Silvia, a shy but intense architecture major at a Lima university, explained her reason for attending the workshop. "I have many concerns related to writing, but my greatest desire is to learn how to relate my evangelical faith to current issues," she wrote. "I want to take up the challenge, which faces evangelicals, of addressing themes like politics, art, sociology, the economy, and Marxism. Until we can speak meaningfully to these issues, our message will not be coherent with reality."

I save another quote similar to Silvia's that stokes my passion to work harder for the development of Christian writers in every country and culture. Wambura Kimunyu, an International Bible Society staff member in Kenya and aspiring novelist, wrote, "At present, foreign literature floods our [African] markets. Our local books, often substandard in authorship, production, and quality, cannot compete effectively with those abroad. What I want most for my country and continent is that we would grow a thriving, independent publishing industry that caters not only to the unique needs of the continent but tells the story of Africa to the ends of the earth. I long for the day when, placed side by side with books from the West, African books would hold their own, telling the truth, telling it well, to the glory and honor of God's name."

With fresh commitment and vision, and with God's help and resources, that day envisioned by Wambura will come. I'm thankful Kenneth Kantzer started me on a journey to enable Christian authors in hard places of the world, and I trust others will join me. Together may we mobilize an international army of Christian writers. God's kingdom will grow, and Christians worldwide will be enriched as a result.

JOHN MAUST is president of Media Associates International, Carol Stream, Illinois. After writing news for *Christianity Today*, he became a missionary journalist in Lima, Peru. Later he was the editor of *Latin America Evangelist*, published by the Latin America Mission. He travels widely training indigenous writers and directs Litt-World, an international writers' conference. A graduate of Ball State University and Wheaton College Graduate School, John has written three books, *Peace and Hope in the Corner of the Dead*, *New Song in the Andes,* and *Cities of Change.*

Part Two: Innovation Solutions

6

Innovation in Content

Jon Hirst

Imagine you are a ministry leader driving into the office on a particularly wet day. You shake off your dank raincoat and settle into your office chair in front of the blue hum of your computer monitor. But before you even open your e-mail, someone pops into your office with that "late-breaking news look" and tells you that a nation's government has fallen and with it years of limited access to mission work. Your mind races with the possibilities. For years you have prayed for ministry opportunities, and now a geopolitical window is cracked open.

You are brought back to reality by the telephone. It is a long-time friend at another mission organization who just heard the same piece of news. Being a good networker, he is already mobilizing several organizations to provide aid and ministry resources. He pauses and then asks, "Do you remember that excellent course your team developed in the '80s for Latin America? That is just what we need for this situation." He then begins talking a hundred miles per hour and ends his conversation with, "So you can cooperate with my team on a new version of that training . . . right?" You freeze as you try to remember what office has the file, who developed it, and where it might be sitting at this very moment. You make a loose commitment, hang up, and then start the hunt.

We all relate to "the hunt" in our ministry lives. We find ourselves asking questions like, "Which computer is that file on?" or "What designer did we use to layout that booklet?" This ongoing hunt reveals the key challenge facing all ministries today: how can we present our ideas in lasting and flexible ways? Each of us is working to take decades of our best content materials and put them into a structure that is as flexible as our ministry opportunities around the world.

This chapter will focus on the emerging innovations that answer these challenges. The key term to understand as we wade through the implications of this challenge is content infrastructure. It means the strategic and technical foundation that allows our ideas to be shaped into useful forms based on the felt needs and requirements of our receivers. Their perception of content has moved from a reliance on traditional content developers to a desire to use content based on their own preferences. In good modern Internet form, we will refer often to those receiving our content as "users." This term provides an umbrella for all the people who will be interacting with your ideas as they take new shapes and meet distinct needs.

If we looked at nonprofit organizations from the 100,000-foot level and scanned their voluminous libraries of content, we would be most impressed. We would see periodicals, books, lesson plans, devotionals, commentaries, lexicons, courses, and much more. Each one would have its own testimony of impact, insight, and usefulness in the Christian community around the world. Some content serves evangelism, and some focuses on discipleship or leadership or theology. Whatever the subject, we have assembled an impressive array of information over the recent centuries. And no wonder. Didn't the abbeys and churches store and copy most of the content that we have from generations gone by? Didn't the printing press begin its long history by printing the Bible?

Walking on Egg Shells

On the surface the status of Christendom's content looks very stable, but underneath is a serious issue that must be confronted. Imagine decades or centuries of content information and materials being stored and developed using a myriad of different formats and strategies. Imagine all of the books that exist only in a few old printed copies. Imagine all of the sermons that only exist in faded manila envelopes. How about the years of articles that are stored in old software that cannot be opened on any modern computer. All these scenarios are simply the tip of the iceberg.

However, the surface can be deceiving. This is in itself a huge frustration because we want so much to believe that the surface is a true indicator of what lies beneath. This is the case with the innovations in content infrastructure.

When I visited the swarming streets of Manila, Philippines, I realized some facts about many countries around the world that I did not want to recognize. As I talked with people about the government systems, communications infrastructure, and other key components to any modern society, I realized that while it looked impressive on the surface, under that very thin veneer of modernity was a jumble of pieces from many different eras all working overtime to meet the demand of this growing city. I don't say this because I think that what many of these countries have developed in spite of insurmountable odds is unimpressive. But as I thought about it more, I realized that many places where I have spent time have the same problem. We fly over the impressive capital cities and feel that all is well, only to find that underneath the panes of glass coating each skyscraper, there are serious infrastructure issues.

Innovation in Mission

Countries with tremendous wealth have a similar problem, but their shell is of a different nature. When we scan modern Western suburbia, or other redeveloped towns in older parts of the world, we see something that is very orderly and proper. However, underneath is a system teeming with all the problems that come from having too much money and no less sin. The shell looks white, but the egg yoke inside is a much different color.

Our nonprofit mission situation is not unique. The entire publishing industry and other content-rich markets are struggling with the same dilemma. The only difference is that many of them have their bottom lines riding on the usefulness of their content and have been quicker to innovate and look at content in new ways.

This is the challenge that all mission organizations currently face. It is easy to identify, but its solution is complex. We live in a world where data is consumed in new and dynamic ways. However, we are not prepared to provide our content in the form that is demanded of us. Furthermore, we cannot mobilize our content for the new ministry outlets that we are yearning to jump into.

The Repurposing Revolution

Our economy's new focus on information produces a record amount of new content. At the same time, there is an amazing thirst for our older content to be pushed into new venues. The concept that makes this possible is called repurposing—when content that was developed for one media or format is retooled for use in another format.

This concept has challenged one of the great communication theories of late twentieth century: "The medium is the message." Nicholas Negroponte, the Wiesner Professor of Media Technology at the Massachusetts Institute of Technology and founding chairman of MIT's Media Laboratory, made an important observation in a 1993 article that helps us to understand the innovative impact of repurposing content. "Marshall McLuhan was right about the medium being the message in the 1960s and 1970s. But that is not the case today. In a digital world the message is the message, and the message, in fact, may be the medium."

There are two reasons for the major push to repurpose content. The first is that the initial format in which content was cast is not sufficient. It is only one of many possible forms that this valuable piece of information could take. If the content was a book, a publisher developed it with technology tools that are common in the publishing industry. If the content was a sermon, a pastor developed it with a wide variety of tools common to the average minister (anything from note cards to PDAs). These formats become a significant roadblock when someone wants to use the content for a purpose other than the specific intent for which it was developed.

The second reason for the push to repurpose content is that users around the world are changing their consumption patterns. Instead of looking at content as an end product that must be dealt with based on the decisions of authors, publishers, and content owners, they are demanding that content be customized and delivered based on the user's needs and preferences. The success of Apple's iPod is just the latest example of the insatiable nature of our on-demand culture.

This change is significant because it means that you, as the content holder, might have the right content to meet a need, but it may not be used because you have not made your content flexible enough to fit into the consumption patterns of the people who have the felt need. With this change in the wings, content developers are searching for easy ways to repurpose content based on people's desires to access information instead of simply buying products.

Our problem is that most of our content is not in a format that allows it to be dynamic and customized for the ever-changing consumption patterns that are driven by our user's felt needs. So while Ministry A might have a wonderful study on church planting in urban areas, it may not be repurposable into a format that current church planters need. For instance, the study might only exist on microfiche. Or the digital document may be lost, and the only remaining copy exists in a library in Oxford, New Delhi, or Houston. This means that it is useless even though it is theoretically very useful.

As I talk to many ministry leaders around the world, this scenario pains them because of the time and resources invested in their content. Our mission world has invested millions of dollars in content development over the years and holds an impressive array of digital assets. However, in the past, content was not viewed as it is today, and so the systems were never put in place to ensure its move into the next generation.

A Changing Ministry Context

The issue of a changing content infrastructure surely speaks to the larger changes going on among mission organizations. Our organizations are moving from an infrastructure like a steel mill to one that looks more like a professional services organization. Richard Tiplady describes the future of ministry organizations in the following way: "A postmodern organization is one that places a high premium on knowledge creation and conversion. One of the ways of dealing with the problems of uncertainty in both our context and in the tasks required of us is to create an environment that values experimentation, creativity and innovation."[1]

The key to understanding the concept of content infrastructure is to imagine the frame of a house. The frame serves as the backbone to all of the other construction elements. In the world of content there are systems and software packages that have the same function. They are called by several names, but the most common way to describe them is Content Management Systems (CMS).

Innovation in Content

We live in a world where content is based on a distributed model. This means that the physical location of the content is not as important as the network to which it belongs and the tools available to access and repurpose that piece of content. Jeremy Rifkin, author of *The Age of Access*, writes about this move to a focus on access and describes the change this way: "The shifts from geography to cyberspace, industrial to cultural capitalism, and ownership to access are going to force a wholesale rethinking of the social contract. . . . In this new worldview that trades in information and services, in consciousness and lived experiences, in which the material gives way to the immaterial and commodifying time becomes more important than expropriating space, the conventional notions of property relations and markets, which came to define the industrial way of life, become increasingly less relevant."[2]

So as we ease into a distributed economy, we face a rising need by those who minister with us and those to whom we seek to minister for customized and felt-need driven content. This need grows stronger as we see the opportunities open to us and are frustrated by our inability to develop the "just in time" resource needed to best communicate our messages.

As a writer and facilitator, I did not easily realize the thin veneer of our mission content world. It was like admiring the detailed stonework in an Italian bistro's entrance, walking through the front door, and realizing that the stonework was really only cheaply painted plaster. In no way do I want to disparage anyone working with these invaluable libraries of ancient and modern content. For me it was like an alarm clock in the middle of the day—curious and particularly effective. Innovation is not trying to sabotage or destroy an existing system or strategy. True innovation comes out of a deep respect for the existing system and a desire to see it survive and thrive as our world changes.

As I began working with organizations around the world engaged in the preservation, development, and repurposing of content, I realized that a new paradigm was needed. Several opportunities developed as I have researched this key innovation. The first opportunity to test it came with a unique project for an association called the International Forum of Bible Agencies (IFOBA: www.ifoba.org). This is an association of Bible translators and distributors focused on advancing the global Bible cause, which is the effective translation and distribution of Scripture to the peoples of the world. We called it the Bible Repository Project, and it is a prototype focused on finding a way to make minority-language Scripture dynamically repurposable for a variety of ministry purposes.

The second project involved helping the Link Care Center, an organization that provides counseling services to missionaries and pastors around the world, develop a model of repurposing their extensive situational management knowledge into online learning opportunities.

Both of these projects have been challenging journeys that I believe provide a guide and example to many other sectors of our ministry community working with content around the world. The rest of this chapter will focus on the key steps that I believe every content developer and holder should walk through as they begin to move their content into the next generation of utility.

Understanding the Commitment

Before starting a project to develop content infrastructure or a content management system, it is absolutely essential to identify the organization's commitment level. There is no doubt that the CEO or director will say that content is important, but how important is it? We all know the reality of new opportunities in a difficult budget year with staff limitations. It is not enough for the leaders to simply say that safeguarding the organization's content is important. The project will never be completed if it is a casual recognition.

There are at least four levels of commitment in organizations today:

1. **Core Value Commitment**: An organization has content development and uses it within their core values. All team members face this issue as they carry out their distinctive roles.
2. **Administration Asset Commitment**: An organization has leaders assigned to content development and maintenance.
3. **Outsource Dependent Commitment**: An organization has valued partners that develop and maintain content and keep content concerns in front of the leadership team.
4. **No Organizational Buy-In**: An organization that does not see the value of content and is not willing to invest in its continued development and maintenance.

Understanding the Need

How do the internal and external audiences use content? Unless leaders understand this, then the infrastructure they develop may not be able to deliver content in a way that their audiences will want to consume it. There is no replacement for research and testing. IFOBA developed the Bible Repository Project with two initial formats to view the Scripture: PDF and HTML. This was done so that they could test its value to their audiences and watch how different audiences used the different formats.

One question that we did not fully master was which formats would be most useful for the test. IFOBA selected PDF and HTML based on some internal justifications, but, in hindsight, it would have been wiser to research which formats would be most useful to their test markets, instead of deciding on the formats internally.

Take a ministry team that writes children's discipleship materials. They work to develop a content infrastructure. They should first identify how people want to use their materials. They might try a written survey or simply make some calls to churches or organizations that are invested users of their content. Most likely, these folks would be happy to explain the most practical format this content could take for their ministry.

Creating a Content Inventory

As we began the process of repurposing Scripture, we immediately ran into the formatting roadblock. For years Bible translators have used a system called SFMs (Standard Format Markers) to encode their texts. Encoding simply means to format the text with bold, indentations, paragraph breaks, and the like. Many of the texts were in excellent condition, and the repurposing process was fairly straightforward. However, other translators used the codes differently, and some didn't use them at all. To further complicate the situation, some translations were proofed and edited in the page layout program instead of in the original encoding. This meant that the SFM file was not the final Bible but only a draft. Also, many different page layout programs were used to produce the final format—a book.

To begin, we created an inventory of how content was kept. This inventory can be very informal or a formal document designed to help others in the organization to understand the content status. We identified the most common formats, the rationale for using each format, and the desirable format that should serve as the cornerstone of the content infrastructure.

Defining Your Foundation

Once their inventory is completed, leaders can begin researching and defining the base structure or format of their content. This format needs to have two main qualifications. First, the infrastructure should correctly describe the content. Describing content is called metadata, which means data about data. The format chosen to store all of the content should allow it to describe the data accurately. This means that an organization describing Sunday school materials should include im-

Innovation in Content

portant things such as grade level, Scripture topics, and the material's language. Metadata can really be anything that helps a ministry describe, categorize, and navigate the data. It is much like a library card catalogue with every piece of content the organization wants to track. The most widely accepted set of metadata that you can freely use for your content is called The Dublin Core Metadata Initiative (www.dublincore.org).

Second, the format should be one that is easy to repurpose into the formats that the ministry decides are key for its purposes. For instance, if all the content needs to be available as PDF files, Quark documents, and Microsoft Word documents, then it will be crucial for the format to allow for that. It is important to note that the initial desires might not form the complete list. For example, it may become important to convert PDF files into PowerPoint files. Does the system you are setting up have that flexibility?

As we researched the format to select for the Link Care and IFOBA projects, we looked in three key places. We looked at what publishers were moving to; we looked at the formats that the software programs were racing to support; and we looked at what innovative content developers were using. The answer was unanimous. They were all using something called XML. (For more information on XML, please see the Resource Library at the end of this chapter.)

Since this isn't a technical book, we will make the definition as basic as possible. In any piece of content, there are three basic components: structure, data, and presentation. XML is a format that separates data from presentation and structure. This allows the data to be pushed fluidly into many different presentations, unlike trying to open your PowerPoint document in Excel.

This foundational decision had major implications for our project. It changed the structure of the content, how the content was designed and broken down, and how the software was developed to input the content. Because we were developing data separate from presentation, we had to create small pieces of content that could be matched up with a number of other pieces in order to be repurposed.

Link Care did this by breaking up all of the situational management learning content into life stages and life situations that contained series, which were made up of steps. These steps could actually be associated with any series or life stage or situation based on the repurposing necessary. So a step about recognizing depression could actually be repurposed into a variety of life stages without being recreated.

Developing a Prototype

Once the foundation is selected, it is necessary to take some of the content and develop a prototype around it. Many call this process rapid prototyping. Instead of developing a product after the idea is fully conceived, it is wiser to develop a skeletal version of the product and do further testing and analysis. If the analysis shows that the idea is on target, then continue developing onto the skeleton. However, if after using and testing the prototype, there are serious problems, then you have not made a major investment. You can turn around, go back to the plans and rethink the parts that are not working properly.

The Bible Repository Project is an example of a rapid prototype. With such a new and experimental idea as dynamic repurposing of Scripture, leaders did not want to move forward with a costly and laborious full launch of a system. At the same time, they needed to see how this idea would actually work and get people trying it. The prototype has been a tremendous success in that goal. Member organizations have had the opportunity to move some of their Scripture into the prototype and think through the different implications to their ministry. They have also identified the problems and challenges that they had not even imagined until they were allowed to actually try it. This project is still in the prototype stage.

Solidifying the Strategy, Documentation, and Requirements

With the prototype working and giving testimony to either the validity or the difficulties with the new infrastructure, leaders can solidify their strategy and begin building the documentation and requirements necessary to launch their new content platform.

The documentation is critical. It should include the following components:

- A clear description of the research, prototype, and results for both internal and external groups.

- A declaration and explanation of the return on investment (ROI) and return on mission (ROM).

- A full feature set that explains all the necessary functions and features that are crucial to the complete infrastructure.

- A sustainability analysis that indicates opportunities for revenue, sources of funding, and sustainability through cost savings.

- An adoption strategy that details how the infrastructure and accompanying tools can be rolled out within the internal and external audiences so as to assure success.

The documentation and requirements will be critical for several key audiences. As we have found with every project we have worked on, there is no project that does not have skeptics, and there is no organization that is not balancing the financial and structural implications of multiple infrastructure projects.

Documentation is critical in the internal marketing efforts that can help with adoption if leaders are caught in the middle of a significant project, such as I am describing. Many projects have been torpedoed after much work has been invested because the project's guardians did not take the time to market its value internally. This whole area of internal marketing is not new. Lynn Upshaw explains the challenge in this way: "It is commonly believed that the sole role of marketing is to sell products and services *outwardly* to customers. In fact, the first and most urgent job of marketing is often to sell *inwardly* toward a company's people. For, it is only when the people of the company fully understand and are committed to the value proposition of the organization and its brands that external marketing can reach its full potential."[3]

Creating a Data Conversion Strategy

Before the final content infrastructure is in place, there must be a plan for data conversion. Imagine someone building a huge house with hundreds of rooms and giving no thought to the furniture or appliances that would go in it. Many times this is exactly what happens in mission organizations. They get caught up in the big project and forget that it is a house for their content.

Usually, in these projects we will be moving old content into a new and standardized format. This will take time and effort that ordinarily is not available. But unless someone can do it effectively, there will be no value for all the work put into your beautiful new house.

One example of this came with the Link Care project. We developed the prototype infrastructure and worked tirelessly on the design and the software, but we did not make a plan that would allow busy Link Care staff to take the time needed to convert materials into the format we could use. So we had a house with no furniture. However, we were just working on the prototype, and they were able to begin buying furniture long before the launch of the full project.

There are two ways to do data conversion: either you manually move content into the new format or you build software that takes your old format and converts it into the new one. The first is usually done in special data-conversion shops located mostly in Southeast Asia, Latin America, Eastern Europe, and the former Soviet Union. The Bible

Repository Project is a good example of the second method. Because most Bible agencies were using a basic structure for encoding Bibles, we were able to build a software tool that took the old encoding and transformed it into the new standard. Of course, different content requires customizing the software tool, but it was built to make the customization process relatively easy. This tool has allowed whole Bibles to be moved into the new standard much more quickly, thus making them available to fill the prototype infrastructure.

Initiating a Content Development Strategy

While the data conversion looks into the past, the content development strategy looks into the future. With this new content infrastructure in place, you need a way to feed the machine. Few people realize, until they make the transition to dynamic content repurposing, that the new consumption patterns require constant content development. Unless you have a strategy to fuel the infrastructure, the wheels will stop turning. Content acts very much like oil in a car. If the oil is not maintained and refreshed regularly, the performance of the car suffers and ultimately fails.

There are some easy steps to take to develop a content development strategy:

- Identify who the content developers are and train them how to write within your new system. Make sure they help you develop the strategy, and walk through the whole process so that you have their approval and input. They are like Jiffy Lube (the North American oil-changing business). They can keep the oil fresh and the car running smoothly. But if they are not well-invested in the process, they might just throw away your engine cap or forget to tighten the oil filter.

- Chart the content development process. Once you have buy-in from your content developers, give them a streamlined and

- well-documented process to follow. They need to know that there is an easy way to get their content into the software system quickly and correctly.

- Build checks and approvals into the system. One of the first things to deteriorate with dynamic and fluid systems is the editorial quality. Just because a content developer can upload content and make it available to your audiences doesn't mean the developer should do this. You can build the infrastructure to require content approvals and checks that will keep the look, feel, and quality there.

- This will require a coordinator or editor as part of the software. However, if you do not include such a person, you will be tainting the entire content pool. The greatest danger to a fluid and dynamic content infrastructure is bad work. Once it gets in, it is sometimes very difficult to pull it out again and do damage control. Within a matter of days, many people could have seen that one piece of content in a variety of formats and contexts.

Conclusion

One of the critical challenges for mission agencies in this new century is the mobilizing of their content for the next generation of consumers. This process is not only critical for those reaching the post-literates of the United States and Western Europe. It is also increasingly important for the dense urban populations in every country. The forces of globalization and its focus on customized and dynamic solutions are shaping even rural content consumers around the world. Imagine the Chinese worker who spends all day watching the machines that stamp out plastic cell phone covers. We are fooled if we think that even at that level, he is not altering his worldview that says, "I can choose how I will accept and consume information."

We must move quickly to deal with the infrastructure challenge instead of simply applying another coat to the surface. If we are willing to accept the change in how content is perceived, then we can prepare our organizations to deliver the good news in formats that these changing audiences will treasure and respect.

Resource Library

Understanding the Importance of Data and Information

1. *E-content* magazine: http://www.econtentmag.com
2. *Business 2.0* magazine: http://www.business20.com
3. Content Management Resources: http://www.krupinski.com/cms-resources.html

Understanding XML

1. Introduction to XML: http://xml.coverpages.org
2. Open Scripture Information Standard: http://www.bibletechnologies.net
3. XML News: http://www.xml.org
4. XML Glossary: http://www.softwareag.com/xml/about/glossary.htm

Content Management Systems

1. Defining Content Management Systems: http://en.wikipedia.org/wiki/Content_management_system
2. CMS Watch: an unbiased review of Content Management Systems: http://www.cmswatch.com/
3. CMS News: http://www.cmswire.com/

7
Innovation in Media Missions
Kurt Wilson

In order to understand the innovations and join the effort of media missionaries, we must understand the unique perspectives and values they hold. This chapter will start with an overview of the mindset of the media missionary, then move to the spiritual foundation of the media mission field, and conclude with the principles of powerful media outreach.

Mindset of Media Missionaries

The mindset of the media missionary rests on a deep appreciation for the scope and, especially, the power of the media. Those who effectively work within this industry have overcome one of the great inconsistencies of the North American mind regarding the media, which I'll illustrate with the following mock debate.

Picture a congressional hearing in one of the stately rooms at the Capitol in Washington, D.C. Congressmen are lined up behind their long table with microphones and pitchers of water. Facing them are expert witnesses from two different industries of considerable influence and success. First to testify are leaders of the advertising industry, an industry now representing over two hundred billion dollars a year in worldwide spending. Second to testify are leaders of the pornography industry, which also generates billions of dollars and boasts more retail outlets around the country than McDonald's. The question they need to answer is simple: Does the media influence behavior?

Leaders from the advertising industry answer a zealous yes. Their confidence flows from a single fact: the businesses they serve would not spend a single dollar on advertising if they didn't believe that the words and pictures they so carefully develop do, in fact, influence behavior. Furthermore, advertising doesn't influence peripheral behavior, it guides one of the most personal and protected areas of our lives—how we spend our money. Advertising executives have reams of case histories to demonstrate that words and pictures influence behavior so effectively that it is a good business investment to spend the average of 300 thousand dollars to produce a single thirty-second advertisement and several times that to have it broadcast. These huge sums are spent year in and year out because they generate substantial profits. The advertising industry is built and continues to grow on the foundation that media messages influence behavior in both significant and predictable ways.

Leaders from the pornography industry, in our mock debate, jump to their feet to refute this testimony. They know that if people truly believed that words and pictures predictably and consistently influence behavior, then they should share responsibility for sexual assault, child abuse, and divorce. When it comes to pornography, or any other destructive media product, they offer a familiar, three-prong defense: it is constitutionally protected free speech; it is simply entertainment (that is, harmless fluff); and, finally, behaviors like rape or abuse flow from such a complex web of decisions and personal history that it is impossible to establish the specific responsibility of media messages.

Thus, the inconsistency of the North American mind prevails; one industry flourishes because the media clearly influences behavior and the other because its influence is so vague. The mindset of the media missionary is not clouded by this inconsistency but is rather informed by the important truth it illustrates: the media predictably and clearly influence the behavior of groups but exert a vague and unpredictable influence over specific individuals.

Understanding this truth allows media missionaries to harness the power of the media for good. Consider the example of Mel Trotter Ministries, a gospel rescue mission in Grand Rapids, Michigan. Like most rescue missions, the majority of their donations come from direct-mail support. Several years ago they received an average of two dollars in donations for every one dollar spent on their mailing efforts. After three years of strategically using television commercials, billboards, newspapers, and public relations, the response to their mailings grew to twenty-nine dollars per donation for every one dollar of cost. These numbers demonstrate that the same power that has increased sales of hamburgers and sodas is also available to help people in need. Those people that used their strategic and artistic skill on behalf of Mel Trotter Ministries were serving as media missionaries, ambassadors for the "least of these" within the broad community that motivated a broad group of people to respond and help.

The mindset of the media missionary also recognizes the media as the environment of our minds and souls. Just as our bodies breathe air and eat food, so too our minds and souls ingest words and images. Like clams at the bottom of the bay, our minds and souls filter the words and images that they live in and spontaneously extract both the nutrients and toxins. Given this real and broad-scale power, media missionaries simultaneously produce media that help influence the community toward good as well as work to clean up the media environment we live in.

Spiritual Foundation of Media Missions

The spiritual and biblical foundation for media missions flows from the opening verses of the Gospel of John: "In the beginning was the Word, and the Word was with God, and the Word was God. He was with God in the beginning. Through him all things were made; without him nothing was made that has been made" (John 1:1–3). The Christian worldview is founded on the concept that the intangible Word of God spoke all of the tangible reality around us into being. This worldview is in sharp contrast to the Darwinian evolutionary understanding, which begins its creation narrative not with the intangible but rather with the tangible—physical matter exploding with the Big Bang.

The distinction between the creation narratives is deeper than the fact that one acknowledges God and the other does not. The Christian worldview sees intangible, spiritual reality as more powerful than the physical reality we can touch because the spiritual reality came before the physical reality and is responsible for the existence and shape of everything in our world.

People who undermine the importance of the media because it's "just entertainment" or "doesn't contribute to the real needs of humanity" miss a core truth from the Scriptures: words and pictures are instruments of the spiritual world, and the spiritual world shapes the physical world.

Unfortunately, words and pictures can be harnessed for the dark side of the spiritual world as well as the light. Consider Nazi Germany: the German people did not suddenly wake up one day and find themselves participating in the evils of the Holocaust. Instead, over the course of a prolonged period, their media were filled with Nazi rhetoric. The people ingested Hitler's impassioned speeches, parades, and other media events that glorified the Aryan race and vilified others. Over the course of time, many Germans (and others across Europe) were involved in evil actions because their minds and souls had first been filled and shaped by the evil of the Nazi message. After World War II a profound and shocked regret settled over Germany as people wondered how their industrious, educated, and historically Christian country could stray so far from the path of goodness. The influence of the media is, clearly, part of the answer.

Another, more recent example of the spiritual power of words for evil is equally clear. The awful genocide and human suffering in Rwanda in 1994 was preceded by the seizing of the national radio broadcast facilities and the broadcasting of ethnic hatred. These broadcasts lasted for several weeks before the actual killing started. The evil worked out in the physical reality of Rwanda was led and shaped by the evil that was broadcast. Because of the spiritual foundation of the media and its ability to be an instrument for good or evil, media missionaries keenly feel the weight of the responsibility they carry.

Principles of Effective Media Missions

God is naturally quite aware of the spiritual significance of words and pictures. Because of this he took great care in the crafting and artistry of his tabernacle:

> "Then Moses said to the Israelites, 'See, the LORD has chosen Bezalel son of Uri, the son of Hur, of the tribe of Judah, and he has filled him with the Spirit of God, with skill, ability and knowledge in all kinds of crafts—to make artistic designs for work in gold, silver and bronze, to cut and set stones, to work in wood and to engage in all kinds of artistic craftsmanship. And he has given both him and Oholiab son of Ahisamach, of the tribe of Dan, the ability to teach others. He has filled them with skill to do all kinds of work as crafts-

men, designers, embroiderers in blue, purple and scarlet yarn and fine linen, and weavers—all of them master craftsmen and designers'" (Exodus 35:30–35).

The context of this passage speaks to the longing in the heart of God that his eternal truth be translated into words, pictures, and stories. He knows that when we can see symbols of his truth and love, the facets of his character that these represent will penetrate our souls and shape our lives in unique ways. As a more recent example, consider the line from Eric Lidell in the Academy Award-winning movie *Chariots of Fire*: "When I run, I feel God's pleasure." That scene, that simple, short line has helped thousands of people more fully grasp the love of God and his yearning for our fullness.

Bezalel and Oholiab were the original media missionaries, called and empowered by God himself to use the media of their day (images woven into the cloth of the tabernacle and carved into the holy implements) to communicate God's love for his people and his abiding presence in their midst.

From this account we draw the first principle for media missions: Media missionaries must be specially gifted by God to be able to carry out the calling with the excellence that glorifies him. Many Israelites likely would have loved that job—developing artistic creations out of gold and fine cloth and serving the living God. This would have been much more exciting and rewarding than tending flocks or gathering manna. But sincere desire or attraction to the prestige doesn't seem to be part of the selection criteria God used. Along these lines, much of the embarrassing media completed in the name of God seems to flow from one of these two foundational problems: it is either produced by sincere people who, nonetheless, lack the artistic talent or background, or it is produced by people seeking power and prestige over true kingdom service.

The second principle is closely related: Beyond just raw, God-given talent and call, effective media missionaries must have training and experience. The mass media is the essence of the broad culture, while evangelical Christianity is a subculture. This inherent cultural divide is at the root of many ineffective media-outreach efforts. Just as Bible translators invest years of linguistic and cultural studies before going to a remote tribe, and several more years in daily interaction before beginning a Bible translation effort, so too the media missionary needs deliberate and adequate preparation in the media culture to be effective.

As the Christian community increases its engagement with the media, more Christian education options are being developed. For example, Biola University and Calvin College are rapidly expanding their film and media training and attracting seasoned professionals to lead their programs. Additionally, the Compass Academy, a relatively young organization in Grand Rapids, Michigan, is dedicated to the training and equipping of media missionaries. It provides hands-on film experience across the whole spectrum of film production. However, the aspiring media missionary shouldn't limit his or her search to options within Christian circles (for reasons I'll more fully explain below). Other respected programs such as Full Sail in Orlando or the leading film schools of Los Angeles or New York provide the required training and network.

Formal training is the first step of preparation that leads to the second, more crucial step: cultural immersion and language fluency. Cursory, initial knowledge of a language or culture is not sufficient for effective, clear translation of biblical truths to a new language. Furthermore, the effectiveness of a Bible translation is established only if the translated concepts are grasped by the target audience, and, conversely, a translation is a failure if the translators are the only people that understand it. Thus, the work is evaluated by the broad culture, and not within the translator's sub-culture. I am here referring only to broadcast media; there is, clearly, value in various media communications designed for existing Christians or the church itself that encourage and strengthen those within the body of Christ.

Innovation in Mission

Just as there is a distinction between the valuable ministry of a pastor in the United States and that of a foreign missionary, for my purposes of explaining innovations in media missions, I am not considering the production of Christian media as media mission work. Media missionaries craft media messages or work within the media industry (film, television, advertising, radio, or print) in such a way as to bring the light of the kingdom to both the industry and the masses in the broad culture reached by it.

Understanding this perspective is important background to the third principle of effective media missions: The media industry itself sets the bar for what constitutes quality and effective media communications, so even sincere missionaries must work within that context. For example, the ads shown during the Super Bowl football game on television are so broadly respected for their quality that many people watch the broadcast not for the game but for the commercials. At the same time, there's not a person in North America who would draw a blank if I asked, "Have you ever seen a bad ad?" Just as a remote tribe will not be effectively reached by a novice linguist, so too our media culture will not be reached by commercials, films, or other media communications that are universally recognized as bad, regardless of the sincere intentions or great hearts of the people behind the effort. Because of this, effective media missionaries spend years working within the media industry, steeping themselves in the culture and values so that they can produce excellent work.

I have been privileged to get to know and work with many people who spent years on staff at some of the largest ad agencies in the world, crafting media for the accounts of Fortune 500 companies. Because of their background, they are now able to produce advertising and communications for Christian organizations that don't look or feel Christian in the subcultural sense of the word, but are deeply Christian in the underlying message communicated. Their ability to communicate Christian truths without the familiar Christian accent of much Christian media grew from their work within the industry. They gained experience with projects that the industry itself recognized as excellent.

In addition to experience within the industry, I recommend exposure to the various publications and events that surround the industry to gain a full and nuanced understanding of the specific media culture you are interested in. For example, those interested in film should regularly attend film festivals, read industry periodicals, and carefully study the techniques of respected experts. Cultural immersion and training is the core of this third principle for effective media missions.

Crafting Effective Kingdom-Building Visual Communications

After watching and analyzing many Christian communications and comparing them with those I saw in the broad market, I found that many with heart-level impact share certain characteristics. Let me illustrate this concept with the following diagram:

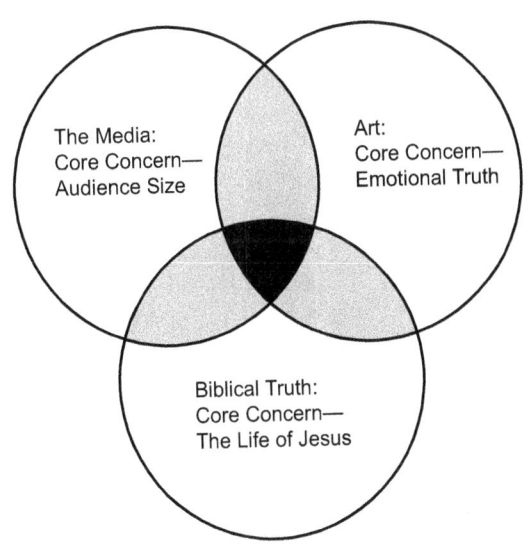

Each circle represents a different sphere of activity, and each sphere is governed by a core concern. The vast world of the media is the first on the left. The industry (including newspapers, magazines, television, radio, and feature films) is driven by the same core concern: size of audience. The media is at its core a business, and maximizing revenue (whether from ticket sales or advertising) requires attracting more "eyeballs" to your content. Because of this reality, we can expect the continued growth of programs utilizing the lowest common denominators of sex and violence. However, kingdom-minded believers need not despair and exit the industry altogether. We simply need to recognize that if we want to reach people in the venue of the media, we need media missionaries that can develop media content that effectively competes in a crowded marketplace and attracts a large enough audience to generate profits.

The second circle of the diagram is the whole art world of theatre, artistic film, music, poetry, painting, and sculpture. While very diverse, like the world of the media, it too has a core concern: emotional truth. Across time and art forms, artists have worked to connect with people on an emotional level, to communicate emotional truth from the heart of the artist to an audience.

The final circle is the whole realm of biblical truth, the heart of what the media missionary seeks to communicate. The core of this sphere of activity is the life of Jesus, the "Word become flesh." The life of Jesus gives us a picture of God himself. This is the foundation and starting place for media communications with eternal value.

The intersections of these circles represent the combination of the core concerns of each sphere, and the very center is the sweet spot for the media missionary: media communications that communicate biblical truth in a way that resonates with emotional truth. Actually accomplishing this in specific communications (and within tight budgets and schedules) is clearly difficult. Crafting sermons or lessons that can effectively reach a person's head is hard enough, but taking that truth to the next level and delivering it in a way that reaches the heart of a broad audience is much more difficult.

Where can an aspiring media missionary start? I recommend two paths: developing stories and parables and developing powerful metaphors.

Developing Stories and Parables

Good storytelling is a powerful art form that has always nourished humanity. All the special effects or technology in the world won't replace its power. Biblical stories, true stories, biographies, fantasies—there are an infinite number of avenues to explore. For inspiration, we can look at the many stories already told within the broad market that resonate with powerful spiritual truths. For example, the widowed Episcopal priest played by Mel Gibson in *Signs* communicates the love and power of God within circumstances of incredible pain more effectively than any sermon I've ever heard—and this movie was a Hollywood thriller, not a Christian film.

Parables are a familiar subset within the world of storytelling. Jesus was naturally the expert, engaging his audience in believable scenarios that communicated important truths to a heart level. While his ministry and communication were largely built around parables, we need to recognize that they are exceptionally difficult to deliver effectively. Viewers can smell a contrived ending or a heavy-handed "moral to this story" from a mile away. The key to an effective parable is that the audience needs to arrive at the intended truth on its own—it can't be all spelled out. While Jesus comfortably risked being misunderstood (or not understood at all) by his audience, followers of Jesus today generally don't tolerate any ambiguity. As a communicator, Jesus demonstrated incredible faith in the Holy Spirit to water and nourish the kingdom seeds he planted. And if we are to use parables effectively, we will need to develop the same level of trust.

Developing Powerful Metaphors

Let me give an example of a powerful mass-media metaphor. A pro-life commercial titled *Seed* opens on a picture of simple gardening dirt and a split screen. Hands come out of each side of the frame and scoop out a handful of dirt and plant a seed, covering the seed with the dirt. Then the hand from the left side scoops back out the seed and dirt, leaving a small hole. As the commercial continues, the right side of the screen alternates between shots of a growing plant and the life of a growing child. All the while, the left side of the screen remains a hole of dirt. The commercial closes with two simple words that resonate on powerful levels because of the power of the metaphor in the commercial: Choose life. Simple metaphors like this can illustrate deep truths and be easily remembered, and they are a good starting place for media missionaries.

In speaking to Peter, Jesus said, "Upon this rock I will build my church; and the gates of hell shall not prevail against it (Matthew 16:18 KJV). Gates, by their very design, are passive and defensive. Gates don't attack. When Jesus said that the gates will not prevail, he assumed that the church would storm the gates of hell, that his church would take the *offensive*, breaking through the gates to take the light of his kingdom into the darkness. What a contrast to the defensive "bunker mentality" of so many Christians.

The good news is that while much of the body of Christ feels under attack, there is a growing number of innovative media missionaries who understand that the light has nothing to fear from the dark. They are confidently taking the eternal truth of Jesus into arenas long ago abandoned by the Christian community.

Certainly, the barriers to effective media outreach are high—exceptionally high, because success flows from a combination of so many factors: gifting, training, preparation, funding, and a great story delivered with excellence. The good news is that a growing number of media missionaries are embracing the truth that Jesus declared—that these barriers, or "gates," will not prevail.

KURT WILSON is the president of Compass Outreach Media, a company in Grand Rapids, Michigan, that provides licenses and customizes award-winning mass media communications to nonprofit organizations around the country. Prior to joining Compass, Kurt spent six years in professional philanthropy, overseeing substantial charitable-giving programs. His involvement with the missionary community began early in his life, as he is a third-generation missionary kid.

8
Innovation in Strategic Planning and Partnerships

Samuel Chiang

Public security officers who had gathered to line up the eager seekers at our booth had left for lunch. The crowd that had twice knocked over our exhibition stall had also disappeared for the midday meal. The organizers of this, the first Comdex show in China, had also vanished to eat. Three hours earlier they had suggested that we stop distributing our software because a crowd formed a line that snaked around the entire convention hall. Presumably, these people were not visiting other exhibits.

We were all very hungry. We had stood in our assigned display booth, right next to the United States Department of Commerce, handing out Bible software CD-ROMs for the last five hours, and we were ready for a break. I suggested lunch. But the businessman from Modesto, California, Derk Van Konynenburg, calmly told me, "You cannot stop now. You don't understand the rules of the harvest."

I was a little taken aback. What did he mean that I did not understand the rules of the harvest? Derk owned a successful, large farming business; so, what were the rules of the harvest? After all, I had already been serving as a missionary, and I practiced the principles of missiology. Little did I realize that God was about to teach me how to apply appropriate technology to the rules of the harvest.

The Odyssey

In the last years of the twentieth century, the French were discreetly leading nations toward European union and the new Euro currency. The Brits were horrified and preoccupied with mad cow disease. The North Americans were building a new wealth bubble with dot-coms and the Internet. Meanwhile, AIDS was spreading unimpeded through many of the African nations. In Asia, China drew both imagination and global attention as an emerging global economic power.

While God is working quietly in Central Asia, North Africa, and the Middle East, he has produced an astounding harvest in China. The size of the harvest is difficult to quantify. A generally agreed upon figure from 1949 suggests there were then 700 thousand Protestant believers. Today, the figure for the overall population of Christians in China is larger than that of 1949 by a factor of at least twenty,[1] and plausibly even one hundred.

China currently has over 100 million Internet users, and over 380 million mobile phone users.[2] But even with advanced technology and economic growth, China's huge Christian population lacks trained leaders. Many large congregations have 3,500 believers for each trained leader. In some places the ratio is over eleven thousand believers to one pastor.[3] Moreover, a critical shortage of printed materials for Christian laity and pastors, combined with the advancement of indigenous and foreign cults, has provided a formidable challenge to the growth of the church. This is further complicated by an urbanization process that divides rural and urban Christians. In this context how can we serve

Innovation in Strategic Planning and Partnerships

alongside church leaders in China and engage in the harvest? How do we apply appropriate technology to serve this large rural and urban audience?

In 1996 I first dreamed of installing on personal computer (PC) desktops and laptops the Chinese simplified script[4] Bible, systematic indigenous and translated curricula, references and charts, hymns, children's animated stories, breathtaking photos of the Holy Land, and devotional books and sermons. All of this would be supported by a robust database, a swift search engine, and agile printing capabilities for mass reproduction—all delivered on CD-ROMs for the church in China. This was to be a conversational journey on strategies, alliances, and partnerships. It was to be a journey of learning. We did not get everything right the first time around (or the second time, for that matter). We learned about ourselves and one another, and we grew. But most of all, we learned about God and his tender mercies. This is a story about building capabilities and innovations in which God created a pathway to the future.

Scan! Scout! Steer!

In a developing nation like China, many projects (ranging from microloans to mom and pop stores; to orphanages, social welfare, and education; to electronics factories, and even semiconductor plants) can entice organizations, churches, or individuals. Many projects may involve technology—even community development projects. One may not think about community development as technology driven, but it is highly integrated. Consider this: the success of a goat project that depends on legumes for feed and de-worming of the goats, and the success of a pig farm project that depends on successful artificial insemination. These projects taught me that the general success of any project requires the right people with the right knowledge.

But God seemed to be moving into a high-tech project. While I have had some experience in this arena,[5] I knew I did not have a team that could meet this challenge—especially in "speed to market." Moreover, should we focus on a team that could develop software in-house, or should our team focus on continual assessment of the church and leadership needs in China?

After much prayer, we decided to outsource the software development. But to whom? In the mid- to late-1990s in China, it was not clear how the PC market was going to develop. We lacked facts about pricing and affordability for the masses. It was not clear at the time which technology platform was going to dominate in China.[6] In the West, Java and the Java Virtual Machine was the rage. Developed rightly, it could straddle a number of platforms with extended shelf life of the product.

After introductions to several outsourcing entities, a friend called and introduced Olive Technology, a fledgling software firm based in India. The company's CEO, Joseph Vijayam, was eager to take on the challenge of providing the Chinese simplified script Bible software in Java. After prayerful consideration, God seemed to be pointing to Olive as the outsourcing partner.

In hindsight, this was critical in understanding the rules of the harvest. Through the technology partnership, there was mutual sharing of a common vision and goal—to see the leaders and laity in China strengthened and multiplied. (Only God can put together a partnership that is full of irony. In the geopolitical theater, India and China are not friends, but in the kingdom harvest, God uses kingdom-minded harvesters in India to assist in the training of church leaders in China through a technology project.)

Having settled the outsourcing of software development, our team focused on church laity assessment, leadership assessment, curriculum assessment and development, user interface development, user acceptance assessment, and interactive feedback for software product improvement.

But I still did not have a well-rounded team, and the organization[7] in which I served was skeptical (as would be normal with any innova-

Innovation in Strategic Planning and Partnerships

tive project). Again I prayed, and God brought along the right people with the right knowledge, oozing with passion. For example, he added Kelly Leung and Florence Leong, Koh Bee Tin, then Fibian Kwong and Francis Tong, and Chan Wai-I and Thomas Yip. These people were of various backgrounds from Hong Kong, Macau, Singapore, the United Kingdom, and Canada, but the chemistry was right. Did we have spirited conversations with hard questions? Yes, but this led the process. This team provided the eyes and ears to scan and codify user needs in China.

Having the right team alone is not enough. The organization[8] still must shepherd the process forward. God uniquely placed Chuck Bennett[9] as president in the life of the organization at that time. Any not-for-profit organization engaging in a high-tech software development project that is rooted in mass user acceptance in a foreign culture is inviting risk. But Chuck, a man with a tolerance for risk, thought it worthwhile to do ministry and took on the challenge. Critical to the process were Chuck's consistent questions on meeting the needs of training church leaders in China in a nonformal setting, based on his own hands-on experiences in the movements of people to Christ in Mexico.

God further set in motion two mentors from afar to ask questions and to minister to my soul. Derk Van Konynenburg was instrumental from a business perspective to keep me and the team focused. William D. Taylor[10] questioned from the ministry perspective to keep us on track. God's harvest generally involves his directed participants to keep the focus.

Profile! Partner! Produce!

The challenge in China is the lack of systematic training of shepherds. But how can a software project assist in addressing leadership training and development? Which model of formal or nonformal education do we adopt? How do we separate knowledge into what I know, what I wish I knew, and what I learned? Furthermore, how do we assess classroom learning when the primary form of education in China is lecture and rote memory?

How do we develop leaders by using a software program that is heavy on content but light on role modeling? You cannot. How do we develop curricula that match users' learning needs? What is the best form and combination of educational delivery—through radio, VCR, CD, VCD, DVD, Internet, facilitator, or television set-top boxes with broadband connections? Finally, what is the appropriate user interface for this software when, at that time, computers were not widely used in China?

We did not have the answers, but we sought to find them. We knew we sorely lacked expertise in a number of disciplines, especially in curriculum design and leadership development. However, as we prayed, God provided continual and providential confirmations.

Through the initial phases of the project, God allowed me to meet with people who became partners. For example, I was translating for Dennis Mock[11] when he was on a tour in China. During our conversation about the software project, he told me about the curriculum that God had led him to write over a period of seventeen months. As I focused more intently on the intended audience and the applicability of the curriculum in cross-cultural settings, I realized that God was answering the need for leadership training and curriculum for the software project.

In similar conversations on the vision of suitable curriculum for the software, God also provided Chinese authors.[12] When the church leaders in China requested learning about systematic expository preaching, our team scouted the world over and came up with possibilities. But we did not know how to proceed because various authors and publishers were worried about intellectual property rights, and they wanted a fair chunk of royalties (even though we were not selling the software). We prayed, and God provided a means to contact Stephen Olford.[13] His

Innovation in Strategic Planning and Partnerships

organization agreed to provide all of his expository preaching series, and he allowed us to translate the material with cultural adaptations.

Our family was sent out as missionaries from two churches, one in Toronto and one in Dallas. Prayer and participation were critical components. Having served in the Peoples' Church, Toronto, in the area of music, I was able to go back to professional musicians and request more hymns for the church in China. I was asked, "Why the older hymns? Why not more of the contemporary worship music?" The answer was that the Chinese church has been in a state of revival, and they found the words of the older hymns intensely personal. David Williams, Mark Wells, and Doug Abbott all selflessly provided hundreds of music scores and hymns in Wave, Midi, and MP3 formats.

Through other community development projects, I observed that knowledge seldom resides in one individual; it is usually spread across an organization or a group of specialists. We were learning to integrate multiple teaching and learning styles in the classroom, leadership training, appropriate curriculum, and software delivery. God again confirmed the process. In January 1999 we met with the leaders of Overseas Council. During our conversation, the software project came up, and we openly described the educational process, the translation process with quality control through backwards translation, and the delivery vehicle of the software. They agreed that it was a sophisticated process and affirmed the project, which by that time had gone through two releases.

God taught us that he will provide the right people with passion for the harvest. He will provide both risk-tolerant leaders and mentors to shepherd the process along. He will provide the right partnerships based on common vision and objectives. A lot of people will make offers with conditions, but God actually shakes and sorts out the relationships. He will provide funding based on his timing.

We were ready for our next release of the software, which the team had named FirstLIGHT. Chinese Christians rise early in the morning and kneel with their torsos erect and upright in prayer. The software was named in observation and honor of the Chinese Christian saints who have endured in their walks with God. It was the second to last day in the second month of 2000. The long-awaited vexation on Y2K had vaporized. The funding sources had carried us toward finishing the project, but not the cost of burning the educational delivery vehicle—the CD-ROM. Our team had set a by-faith date of February 29, 2000, for the release. I was anticipating final funding for the project. I asked God where His confirmation was.

At 10:30 in the morning in Hong Kong, the telephone rang. It was Henry Chu from our other sending church in Texas, the Dallas Chinese Fellowship Church. He told me that God had laid a burden on his heart to help on the FirstLIGHT project. He indicated he would help financially. As we parted on the phone, joy flooded my soul.

I knew God had answered and that the software would be released by our faith date. As I left the office for an appointment, I reflected and worshiped God—all while riding in a crowded train system in Hong Kong.

The next day, February 29, at 6:30 A.M., as I was typing a letter describing the release of the software, the project manager of FirstLIGHT, Fibian Kwong, called. As she started the conversation, I interrupted and congratulated her on the successful release. She was both dumbfounded and curious; she wanted to know how I knew. In fact, she asked if the CEO of our outsource partner, Joseph Vijayam of Olive Technology, had called. I told her that no one had called. She indicated that the final version of the software was burned to a glass master copy only at 2:30 on that morning, so how did I know? I knew because God had indicated his provision the day prior, through a call from a friend.

Innovation in Strategic Planning and Partnerships

Refocus! Reiterations! Results!

Releasing the FirstLIGHT software was perhaps the easy part. The issues of technology platform and user acceptance had always loomed as larger questions. For example, we worked carefully with users in China, treating them as full partners in getting feedback on the interface. This is not always an easy matter to manage. Users have opinions (to be respected), and they can be very critical (Christian or not). Yet, this was crucial input for future versions of the software.

At that time in China when the computer market was nascent, we were also trying to determine a technology platform that would intersect the technology path. Although the earliest version of the software was written in Java, we were forced to change course when Microsoft decided to no longer bundle important Java software and capabilities with its Windows operating system. This difficult course-change required us to lay down our egos and entrepreneurialism, refocusing our attention to where the market was headed.

We continually encountered people who wanted to put their material on the delivery vehicle—FirstLIGHT. There were hard choices to make, and these potential partners made their arguments harder still. They tried to convince the team that they were building our capacity; or they were assisting us in fundamentally changing the rules of training in China; or some were fanciful enough to suggest that together we could create and dominate emerging opportunities. Some of the ideas were difficult to sort out, but we constantly went back to the users—church leaders and tentmakers in China.

We consistently asked the question: Will the curriculum content be accepted by both the open churches and also the house churches?[14] We continually monitored the installed base of computers, mobile phones, and television set-top boxes. We continually asked what would bring long-term impact along with a tangible shelf life that would perhaps outlast the project itself. Some people with resources were forever trying to get us to move into the Internet space and called us myopic for not doing so. Others rhapsodized that great vulnerabilities existed if we did not move into the media convergence in the mobile phone market space.

The potential curriculum partners and funding resource partners provided a healthy forum of ideas. However, as with many projects, the keys to results were strategic architecture (major capabilities to be built), technology architecture, scope management, and distribution with feedback plans. God provided mission agencies to assist in the distribution plans as well as many other partnering organizations with a view toward training in China. But particularly helpful were Bill Smith and Lewis Abbott.[15] Separately, they helped us sort through many of the queries and ideas with a view from the end, looking backward. Thus, with prayer and added perspectives, we were able to stay on track and not let certain influences or funding overtake the project. In any kingdom harvest, working with God's churches and patterns is essential in understanding his timing and his methods.

We saw the church in China growing steadily, and we looked toward how to minister to the next generation of youth numbering 400 million[16] who are under age eighteen. There was (and still is) a huge request from China for materials for children and youth. Again, we prayed about this matter. At a missions conference at Shenandoah Baptist Church in Roanoke, Virginia, in 1999, I recalled seeing a video report from the former European director of Child Evangelism Fellowship (CEF), an Irish man named Sam Doherty. A year later I was at the same church speaking at their Saturday morning breakfast, reporting back to the church what God was doing with FirstLIGHT. Afterward, a man with an accent came up and said he had a witness in his heart and wanted to participate in the FirstLIGHT project. This man was Sam Doherty. Thus, the entire CEF curriculum was provided.

God provided the right people with passion, the right partners with common vision and objectives, and the right resources. But, that is

Innovation in Strategic Planning and Partnerships

not all for the rules of the harvest. God provided his surprises and his results.

Providing accountability reports from China is not an easy task, but it must be done. God had provided many means for people in China to whisper about the FirstLIGHT software so that many organizations and individuals outside of China, of whom we had never met nor heard, actually partnered to provide this product because it was requested in China. But how would we know about user acceptance in different circles? We thought we would not. But God surprised us.

One day I was in Beijing in the home of a church leader who once served on the staff of Wu Yi.[17] Having just arrived on a long flight, I was quietly observing several conversations among the intellectuals, including one small group of people who had just received the FirstLIGHT software from their friends in another province. After installation and some time spent working with the software, a member of that group immediately got up and telephoned her brother. She asked if he had seen this software because it was robust, full of resources, and had mass-media printing capabilities. I was delighted to know that among the intellectuals in China, there was recognition of the software's tremendous value. What about seminaries and theological schools? Would they use FirstLIGHT?

In 2001 I was riding in the back of a taxi along with a house church leader and the dean of studies of a Bible institute in one of the bread basket provinces of China. It was my first meeting with the dean of studies. He, in turn, was already well acquainted with the house church leader. In the midst of our conversation, he asked the house church leader if he knew where to get more FirstLIGHT CD-ROMs because professors and teachers were using the materials to teach their students. I praised the Lord for these impromptu confirmations.

As we entered the new millennium, many people brought forth various concepts of kingdom initial public offerings (IPOs). I was not certain that we, in ourselves, could actually do a kingdom IPO. This was strictly of God's choosing, for his purpose, at his timing. God unfolded one more surprise for our FirstLIGHT team.

This team worked tirelessly to manage more than one hundred people, distributed across seven territories and countries, sprinkled on three continents. My role was simply to pray, meet, delegate, cheer on, and be accountable to the sponsors of the project. We focused fully on the laity and church leaders in China. But God had seen fit to bring over two hundred partners to distribute and use FirstLIGHT not only in China but also elsewhere. The Chinese diaspora is a global phenomenon. God had seen fit to accomplish his kingdom IPO by providing the FirstLIGHT software to approximately fifty different territories and countries.[18]

Our life is a journey. The rules of the harvest continue today, and they always have a common beginning—prayer. I shall not forget an episode in one of the earlier releases of this software. After a meeting in Singapore, we stared at the reality of not making the planned release date. Arriving at the beautiful Changi airport, which was full of people, I felt quite alone. I prayed and pleaded with God for us to fall in line and redeem the time.

Soon thereafter, thought after thought came rushing into my mind, and I knew I needed to write them down. So, looking for the nearest thing to me in the airport departure lounge, I grabbed an air-sickness bag. On it, line by line, I wrote the steps and processes that needed to happen for the team to release on time. As I neared the end of list making, it was also the end of the vertical bag. I looked again at the bag and realized these were logical and sequential steps that needed to happen. I praised the Lord. In turn, a hymn rushed into my heart, and this became the theme song of FirstLIGHT—"Thine is the Glory:"[19]

> No more we doubt Thee, glorious Prince of life;
> Life is naught without Thee; aid us in our strife;
> Make us more than conquerors, through Thy deathless love;
> Bring us safe through Jordan to Thy home above.

Innovation in Strategic Planning and Partnerships

SAMUEL E. CHIANG is chief operating officer and international director of planning, strategy, and partnerships for Trans World Radio, Hong Kong. He previously served as East Asia director for Partners International. He is a graduate of Dallas Theological Seminary and also holds a degree in commerce, accounting, and economics from the University of Toronto. Samuel was born in Taiwan and has lived in Canada, the United States, and Hong Kong.

9
Innovation in Resourcing Latin American Pastors

Aaron Sandoval

Latin America is a key area of Christian growth in the world. In fact, the church is growing so fast that it is hard to keep up with it. Discipleship and maturity of believers is the greatest need of this growing body of believers. How do we reach them all? A key element in church growth and discipleship throughout the Spanish-speaking world will be the creation of a content distribution network.

I want to tell you about a friend of mine. Pablo is a pastor in San Pedro Sula, Honduras. He is thirty-two years old, married, and has three beautiful kids. He's working in a small but growing church there, averaging about seventy-five members. Pablo has never had the opportunity to go to seminary, even though he has attended a few ministry conferences and received some informal training. Like a lot of pastors in the area, he has to work a second job to provide for his family. He works as a driver for a distribution company. He rushes home on

Wednesday nights to lead the men's meeting, on Thursday nights for the prayer meetings, and on Saturdays for the youth meetings.

It is now late on a Saturday night, and Pastor Pablo is tired. He has not spent much time with his family this week, and he still has to prepare for the next day's church service. He has no material to use in preparing his message. He is dry, burned out, and it is getting late. Where can he turn?

Because the church in Latin America is growing at a tremendous pace, we struggle to disciple this growing body of believers. Lack of resources, materials, and a common platform are all factors in our inability to provide training or even just basic discipleship.

The Spanish-speaking world is viewed as a gigantic market by many, a mass of people living in huge urban areas, ripe for the harvest. One of the facts that we seem to overlook is that Latin America is divided into eighteen countries, each with its own identity, laws, regulations, cultures, sociopolitical ideologies, and economies. Distribution of materials among these countries is difficult, expensive, and, simply put, a big headache.

Agencies called to provide ministry resources face huge obstacles. The tasks of receiving an order, shipping, billing, and getting paid become overwhelming. While free trade and shared markets are beginning to sprout up throughout the region, logistics are still an obstacle to taking discipleship materials to all corners of Latin America.

One of the effects of this communication difficulty has been the creation of regionalized ministries. There are hundreds, maybe thousands, of healthy, vibrant, growing ministries sprinkled throughout the Spanish-speaking world. I picture them as bright stars in a dark night. While they provide light, very few of them have been able to light up the whole sky.

In the Spanish-speaking world, we lack a common knowledge base. The church in North America is part of society. It was there at the founding of the nation and continues to be a major force. The church

Innovation in Resourcing Latin American Pastors

has been able to take advantage of and participate in the infrastructure that society uses. It is very easy for a believer in one city in the United States to fellowship with one in another city. There is a natural affinity. They both listen to the same Christian shows and music on the radio, and they both read the same books from the same authors. They have all been touched by a variety of different ministries like Focus on the Family, Moody, Broadcasting Network, and others.

This "network," this connection that exists among North American believers, is what I call the common knowledge base. There isn't some huge Christian conglomerate out there making sure that all believers are connected and sharpening each other. It just happens. It is a result of a church that has taken advantage of the infrastructure that society has created. It is just there.

In Latin America we have no such common base. There is no way that two believers, one in Mexico and one in Chile, have much in common. Ministries are regionalized, since logistics are very difficult. Society in itself does not have that type of infrastructure in Latin America. The church must invest in infrastructure that will join together the different parts of the body of Christ and allow for free flow of learning, growing, and sharing.

What then do we do to resource these pastors and leaders? There is a tremendous need for solid discipleship materials, but how do we get them to where they are most needed? In the face of how hard it is to distribute materials, do we give up?

Well, not all is against us in Latin America. We do have certain advantages working for us. First of all, the Latin American community speaks the same language. No translation needs to occur when sharing content. Technology is also on our side. It is no secret that Latin America is booming as far as the Internet is concerned. What's more, it's not limited to urban centers or to the wealthy.

While visiting small towns in the Guatemalan highlands, right next to the town square, I have seen cyber cafes, where a dozen or so people type away, check e-mail, chat with friends, or just surf the Web. In North America we all have computers and can access the Internet from home. This is not so in the Spanish-speaking world. Just like everything else, the use of computers is a social thing. Even in the smallest of towns, cyber cafes have become a common and familiar sight.

So we have a growing church and a need for materials. We realize that we can't just put a whole bunch of books in a box and ship them efficiently. We know material is available, but usually in a regional setting, because we are not able to share across borders.

I thank the Lord for the wisdom he has given various ministries to use technological advances for the sake of the gospel. Organizations and individuals have been able to place ministry materials right in the hands of these pastors, thousands of miles away.

Starting with U.S.-based organizations, ministries have taken resources and, through the Web, delivered them in Spanish across the globe. Youth Specialties (YS) is one example. Having had success in building a resource for youth pastors and leaders from across the country, they have taken their ministry a step further. Moving their material into Spanish and setting up an entirely Spanish-based Web site, YS has now reached millions of Hispanics in the United States as well as made a tremendous impact on youth groups throughout the continent.

Ministries such as *Christianity Today* have also had an impact in Latin America. Using a different approach, they have partnered with visionary ministries in the Spanish-speaking world. Working with DesarrolloCristiano.com, a resourcing ministry in Costa Rica, *Christianity Today* has been able to support the development of discipleship in Latin America.

ObreroFiel.com, a ministry of CAM International, has also made a tremendous impact in Latin America. Taking over one hundred years of ministry material in Spanish online, CAM, through ObreroFiel.com, has been able to help thousands of pastors and ministry leaders throughout the world with their ministry needs.

Pastors in Latin America, Spain, and other countries (ObreroFiel.com has received responses from France, Israel, and Australia) now can access materials that will help in the discipleship needs of the church. When you add to that the number of ministries that have taken this same approach from within Latin America (Web sites such as www.sigueme.com.ar and www.centraldesermones.com), it is exciting to see what God is doing.

While some of these first steps are very encouraging, the journey is far from over. A lot of these pioneering ministries will face difficult challenges as technology continues to develop. They will have to consider strategy, convergence, and infrastructure.

With faster and faster computers being developed and software companies battling each other over shelf space, technology is constantly changing and adapting. What is cutting edge by the opening bell on Wall Street can be obsolete by lunch time.

How do you design a technology infrastructure that can deliver in all of these circumstances? If technology is constantly outdating itself, how can we ever justify an investment in infrastructure? The answer lies in designing a system that goes beyond the technologies that deliver it.

This element is key, even for the business environment. Consider how large software companies don't market their technologies but, rather, the solution to problems. It is not as important to have the latest, coolest software installed; it is imperative to find a solution that delivers regardless of what system you are running.

The dominance of purpose over technology has begun and will continue to rise in importance. People everywhere will have to find a way to deliver their purpose, achieve their goals, and get results. Different technologies merely become tools in the tool chest of corporations.

The same is true of our ministry goals, but even more so in Latin America. The technology gap in Latin America is growing. Some have state of the art computers; others simply have no technology at all. On one hand, we have top of the line technology in hot-spot areas where professionals and businesspeople use their newest equipment. However, a few miles down the road, there are people who barely know how to read. This problem makes strategy a critical consideration. So do we reinvent the wheel every time? Do we develop a strategy that resources some ministries to deal with one segment of the population and others to deal with a different segment?

Would it not be more efficient to develop an infrastructure that delivers solid content regardless of the technology or product that it was accessed with? The technology necessary to create such a project, in theory, would not even be that complicated. It would only need to contain a few elements.

The first element would be the development of database-driven applications, written in some form of extensible or flexible language like XML, and then have it delivered across a myriad of platforms. Technologies like XML are simple ways that allow us to structure data in a way that makes sense. This allows us to organize content in such a way that it can then be distributed on any number of media. We can save an article and have it delivered via a Web page, a printed page, through a cell phone, or any other way we can think of without really having to rework all the content.

This is the same principle used by the travel industry. Airlines need to inform the passengers about schedules, and agencies sell the tickets for the seats. But the whole industry runs off databases and systems managed by one or two companies. All that content is stored and then delivered across different platforms like online travel stores, travel agencies, ticket stands at the airport, and phone purchases.

Another requirement of this type of technology would be the continued development of application platforms to deliver the content.

These applications could be delivered by niche ministries interested in a certain type of communication medium.

The Lord has created the body of Christ as a fully functioning body. The ability to have some of us concentrate on one aspect of ministry and others on a different aspect makes us dependent on each other and allows us to focus on what we are really good at.

Let us allow pastors and teachers to do just that. They need to focus on writing and producing great materials for the edification of the church. We need to let those who have technical abilities develop them and use these tools for the growth of the church. And finally, we need to have a way to link the two of them. By creating a content distribution system, we allow a more focused system in which everyone works together.

How would a network like this actually work? Let's use an example of a youth event. As I was growing up, a campaign was launched to reach the youth in the city of Puebla, Mexico, called *Prioridad* (Priority). We had events, speakers, and activities.

The directors of this event could have stored all their work in a large database. They could have saved their strategic notes on how to attract youth, how to get a good speaker, how to pay for the event, the notes and handouts they gave out, as well as the activity guides. They could then add the contact information of featured speakers, even the music they recorded at the event. All of the items could have been saved in a database.

This content could then be used over and over again by those other than the people in charge of the Priority meetings. Youth leaders all over the Spanish-speaking world could benefit from what these pioneers learned. Others could implement some of the same strategies, use some of the same handouts, and even get in touch with the same speakers.

Content such as this can be repackaged and reused in a variety of ways. Every single item saved to that database can be used as an entity within itself.

Imagine having a Web site for youth pastors that looks in the database and pulls out only the activity ideas. Or, imagine a radio station that can download the music created for Priority and broadcast it. What about a small church in the Andes mountains? Print shops set up to distribute materials there can have access to the content to print lessons based on the content of the event. All of these items when put together create a wonderful event that can be repackaged and used for different purposes in different areas of the world. Technology like this is a reality, and as content based systems like XML become more mainstream, projects like this become more feasible.

When we start to diversify our output of materials, we can also begin to think of convergence. We can't force people to spend all day looking at our technology. We need to realize that we are more efficient if we can deliver our content across a multitude of platforms, whether it is the Web, print, audio, video, or any other. Wouldn't our message be more effective if it was constantly and consistently delivered? As we think about convergence, let's remember that there is power in repetition.

We can envision a leader in a Spanish-speaking church who can download a study on any book of the Bible and, at the same time, receive a Christian magazine that has an application on the same topic. He can turn on the radio and listen to music that deals with the same issues. And, after a while, the message starts sinking in. It is a slow, constant process that uses a mixture of mediums, different platforms on which the same content is delivered in different ways and from different angles.

The organization and choreography necessary to develop such a program would be tremendous. However, if many different platforms were all connected into the same database, accomplishment would not be too far away.

A content distribution system enables sharing and delivery across different media, allowing users to learn the message as they read a book, glance at a magazine, listen to the radio, go to church, communicate with others, and so on. The message then sticks in the minds of those who hear, and the fruit of that message brings about a stronger body of believers.

A distribution system like this doesn't just happen out of circumstance. An investment in infrastructure is required. The study of socioeconomics in Latin America is very interesting. Business seems to be cyclical, and investment in infrastructure is not the exception. Governments invest heavily in infrastructure (roads, electricity, buildings, and so forth), and then run those infrastructure investments dry.

The same seems true of some ministries. Great investments were made in ministry infrastructure in the 1950s and '60s in Latin America. Many buildings were built; radio stations put in transmission antennas; and publishing houses purchased printing presses. Some ministries have used the infrastructure available to them until they couldn't run anymore. At that point, they mixed in a little creativity, a little hot-wiring, and the machine became as good as new. Some ministries have had to be very good stewards of their investments, and the lack of necessary funds has made the continued use of obsolete machinery mandatory.

However, we are entering a new era. As a whole, the Spanish-speaking church needs to make some major investments again in Latin America. New technologies require new investments that will allow a more efficient and more effective spread of the gospel.

Because technologies keep changing at such a rapid pace, it is hard to know what technologies to invest in. The top of the line printer that a company invests in today is hardly worth a half of its price in a few months. The most efficient computers are pathetically slow only a few years later.

So if we are talking about a pattern of investment and then continued use of this technology for a long period of time, it is important to think about technologies that don't evolve so quickly. New technologies like XML were written keeping an unknown growth potential in mind. If we focus on flexibility, then we can consider the design of an infrastructure system that will efficiently and effectively distribute content to the entire Spanish-speaking world.

We are quickly moving toward a content distribution economy. Print-on-demand books is a good example of this. Soon the large publishing houses will no longer depend on their presses and their products to generate revenue. Their economy will be based on the development and distribution of content. That same model applies to our situation in Latin America. If it is so difficult to move our products across this large continent, why not take advantage of new technologies that help us to distribute our content?

There is a great need in Latin America. Churches are starving for materials that produce vibrant, growing believers, but how do we supply them? What can we do? Let's dream big. Let's build big. The development of a creative infrastructure that allows for content sharing is an exciting project. Envision with me a resourced Latin American church ready to reach the world for our Lord.

AARON SANDOVAL grew up on the mission field, exposed to Christian publishing. He is the cofounder of ObreroFiel.com, an Internet tool to resource pastors and leaders in the Spanish-speaking world. He has served as vice-president of the Latin American Internet Network as well as a board member of a Latin American Christian publishing house. He serves ministries through strategy and implementation of Web solutions for fundraising needs as the director of eArchitecture of ITERO!, an online relationship fundraising group.

10
Innovation in Online Learning
Joel Dylhoff

The face of world missions is changing. Mission agencies are redefining the relationships among themselves, sending churches, and emerging churches. In an effort to connect people around the common goal of building the church around the world, technology and communication strategies and methodologies are crucial. If you're reading this book, you're probably one of the people thinking about this.

One aspect of the challenge agencies face is the increased mobility of missionaries brought about by inexpensive transportation. Traveling home to tend to sick family members, attend conferences, and put children in school is readily available and convenient. Missionaries who stay on the field for four years before returning to the United States for a full year of furlough are the exception. The ability of the missions community to send people to difficult locations and to respond to sudden changes in world politics has dramatically increased. Hot spots erupt in countries, and agencies have to decide overnight whether to encourage their personnel to stay or return home. When a crisis erupts, the natural method for agencies to use to communicate their actions and intentions and to disseminate them is via the Web.

Missionary mobility also means that missionaries are apt to move from field to field within a particular agency, depending on the need. These changes present another set of challenges, as missionaries move between cultures, languages, and roles. To respond to these changes, many mission agencies have begun to pay attention to ways of providing training to their people while they remain in the field. This has also become important as agencies have discovered that the predeparture orientation they give people leaving for the field does not always address the situations that arise on the field and cannot prepare people for situations that take place several years after their arrival. One way that some agencies are seeking to provide this training is by tapping into an idea that is already widespread in the business world—delivering on-the-job training using the Internet. Using the Internet to connect learners around the world is a requirement when learners are separated by languages, cultures, and time zones. Learners are also separated from one another by their own knowledge of a particular field. Many people come into mission work as their second or third career and bring with them a diverse array of abilities, life experiences, educational backgrounds, and varying perspectives and understandings of what the task of the missionary is to be. To train these individuals well, both the content and the methodology must be adaptable. People may come to missions with high degrees of competence in other fields but may not have the ministry and cross-cultural abilities needed on the field. Consequently, agencies are looking for ways to provide training for missionaries that not only provides them with training in areas of weakness but also taps areas of strength to help instruct other members of the learning community.

The training needs of the missions community are complex. Consider new missionary recruits. Not only do they need to develop ministerial and relational competencies but they also need to learn the organization's financial systems, goals and values, and other procedural skills. In addition, there is a need to understand the culture, language, church history, and social values of the culture they are entering. Finally, there is a need for continued growth in biblical understanding. Even in this list, various other concerns also surface from time to time that could be addressed by on-the-job training.

Missionaries in the field also have training requirements: further growth in language competence, gaining a more nuanced understanding of the history and culture of the people they are working with, identifying and engaging points of the culture where the gospel can be presented, and growth in leadership and discipling new Christians. Online training can be used in this scenario to train missionaries on the field and to connect them with other people who are studying the same things without leaving the field.

Another advantage online learning provides to the missionary community is the ability to access information that might otherwise be unavailable. For instance, in developing partnerships with colleges and universities, agencies may be able to tap into the online libraries and databases the schools already own, thus opening up entire libraries of information for their learners that would otherwise be out of reach.

Questions about Training

In considering how to train across geographical boundaries, there are a number of questions that arise that need answers. Does computer-based training provide an adequate solution? Is there some way of training regionally in a classroom? Can learning communities be facilitated and, if so, how? Should training be face-to-face? Should it be held at the home office? What things need to be communicated and to whom, and when do they need the information? What are the opportunities for training to take place within the country itself? What sort of infrastructure is needed? What is the cost? What things can be taught online? What things must be taught in a classroom setting? Who determines the curriculum? The deeper we delve into the world of professional training and development, the more questions seem to arise.

Does online training answer any of these problems? Yes and no. Because missionaries are a mobile group of people who may work in places where open communication is unwise, deploying a training system that relies heavily on Internet technology may not be possible for all missionaries at all times.

For example, missionaries working in Taiwan are very likely to have broadband connections in their homes. In addition, many would have access to Web-enabled cell phones with worldwide roaming capabilities and the ability to send and receive messages anywhere in the world. On the other hand, missionaries in Chad may only be able to send and receive e-mail when they are at a central office, via a shared satellite phone connected to an older computer.

Providing training to on-field missionaries in some countries also raises the question of security. Depending on the location of the missionary, there may be restrictions on what can be said openly and how communications between the home office and the missionary can take place. In such cases, developing an entirely Web-based training structure is not effective. The idea that there is anonymity on the Web is a myth. All Web traffic can be and is tracked.

Another critical issue is how to implement effective quality control and accountability for participants. What structures will allow both adequate flexibility and well-guided, focused study? In doing pilot testing for online collaborative learning forums, The Evangelical Alliance Mission (TEAM) found that even among dedicated participants, maintaining continuity throughout the duration of a learning group proved challenging without some system of rewards and accountability in place.

Finally, not all training is effectively taught by any one particular method. Some information can be effectively learned through simply reading it, some through face-to-face instruction, and some through hands-on learning. For example, while a facilitated online discussion about the effectiveness of a particular evangelistic tool among youth may be something that lends itself well to the online arena, learning to speak a new language is something best learned in a classroom setting with face-to-face interaction with other learners and ready access to a knowledgeable teacher.

Online learning is the most recent application of new technology to education and training. Because it takes place online, and not in a face-to-face environment, a different educational philosophy is needed to put together an effective online strategy as opposed to a classroom training program. Regardless, corporations are looking to online training to provide their employees with the training they need. In many cases, the extra cost associated with online learning pays for itself for large organizations in the money saved that would have been spent on travel, room and board, renting a conference area, and the work hours lost in transit. Instead, they invest in hardware, software, and instructional designers capable of producing courses that can be used many times online. Although the training meetings I have described occur less frequently in the missions world than in the corporate world, online learning allows missionaries the opportunity to learn about and apply information produced by any connected member much more rapidly than ever before.

To be successful an online learning program requires instructional design, information technology, Web development, and communications ingredients. Of these, the importance of solid instructional design cannot be overstated. It provides the structure to which technology is applied to develop a useful and effective online learning environment.

TEAM's foray into online learning was prompted by its board's desire to see one of the organization's core values—lifelong learning—developed in a way that would benefit missionaries without being an added burden. From the beginning a number of challenges surfaced: how to organize the groups, what communications technology to use, what educational philosophy to use, how to fund the project, and how to keep the online space secure were just a few of them. These questions had to be answered as the training group tackled the problem.

The first question any organization developing an online learning program needs to answer is, What are we trying to accomplish with the program? At TEAM the goal was to connect missionaries with other people with whom they could study and learn, both within the organization and outside it. In the process of working through this challenge, the work team produced a model of a learning environment robust enough to connect virtually anyone involved in the missions enterprise who was interested in being part of a learning community.

Developing an online learning program can be expensive, both in terms of time and in terms of the hardware and software needed. However, some new solutions and ideas are developing that show promise of lowering some of these costs. Macromedia (now Adobe) has released a number of e-learning extensions for Dreamweaver, which allow Web designers to build online training programs using standard Web design tools. Microsoft's SharePoint Services provides users with collaborative software for exchanging documents and sharing other information. Other companies are moving into the market as well with either competing products or extensions to existing products that increase their power and usability. The costs remain high, however, for those wishing to purchase software that is able to tap all of the options online learning can provide. As the market matures, costs will drop; and as standards are established, the field will begin to stabilize. In the meantime, some software vendors spring up, only to consolidate or go out of business shortly thereafter. Caution is needed when choosing a software vendor.

Those looking to develop an online training program need to consider which of three avenues they wish to pursue when making a decision about software. The first option is to find software that is close to the needs of the organization and customize it. This can be expensive and time-consuming but is likely to result in a final product that satisfies the needs of the organization. The second is to find software that is close to what the organization is seeking to accomplish, implement it as it is, and work around the software where needed. Although not as elegant, this solution can result in less design difficulty and a speedier implementation. Finally, as the industry matures, it is becoming possible to create training elements from scratch, allowing organizations to create learning environments from components themselves, slowly building a comprehensive training program over time.

Developing an Online Learning Strategy

Online learning needs to be integrated into an organization's training plan in order for it to be successful. Online learning cannot solve all of the challenges in training that an organization faces. When developing an online learning strategy, it is important to understand that, in this case, the technology merely extends the reach and availability of the learning and training programs already taking place. Though the technology is new and the philosophy about how best to deploy it is developing, the training it provides is not something new and different—it is a new extension of existing training. Simply using this technology will not fix a poor or flawed training program. It will only increase the scale of the flaw.

For online learning to be successful, it needs to help the organization reach its goals and it must be championed by its leaders. If senior leadership does not see value in the training and development of its members, the project will struggle from the beginning. Online learning should enhance and contribute to the development of the organization, reflecting its values and goals. Roger Luce, Director of the Center for Lifelong Learning echoes this. "Putting together a training program requires 100 percent support from upper-level leadership. Projects like this are not cheap in terms of money or manpower."

Integrating online learning into other types of learning can be done *(a)* by referring to online learning components in other training environments to remind students of the resources available to them and *(b)* by providing material online that supplements the training being conducted using other methods.

Another way of helping learners get involved with online learning is to train them in its use. New technology often brings with it some sort of learning curve, which can be intimidating for first-time users who are unaccustomed to it. By teaching them how to use the software, much of the mystery can be removed, and learners can work with the programs and ask questions in an environment that encourages them to explore.

If approval and support are given by an organization's senior leadership, it is time to assemble the training team. At TEAM the team contained some people with specialized expertise, including an education specialist for missionaries' children, several PhDs with experience in education, and a knowledgeable technology consultant. From the outset, representatives from the following disciplines should be present:

- **Instructional design**: These people provide organization, structure, and flow to the learning. They are the ones responsible for setting the outcomes of the learning and the broad strategy for how to accomplish them. Without these people, there is a significant risk of developing flaws in your training system's strategy.

- **Information technology**: Online learning requires a large amount of data tracking, reporting, and design work. Depending on the strategy chosen, IT work may be needed to customize training software or to develop new training modules. Hardware and software considerations make it important that those responsible for this aspect of training be included on the team to help the group avoid technology pitfalls and to help solve implementation challenges as they arise.

- **Users**: If an online training system is developed to provide on-field training to missionaries, it is critical that their input be sought throughout the process. Not doing this risks building a training system that is either not useful or not accessible to its intended audience.

- **Web specialists**: Because online learning is designed to function on the Web, it is important that the training team include someone with a strong understanding of the Web to guide the group in issues relating to connectivity, security, and online functionality.

- **Facilitators**: Facilitators are critical to making sure that the users have a good experience with the software and other learners. Facilitators need to be warm and friendly in their interaction with the users, able to maintain conversations among participants who may not know each other, and have enough knowledge of the learning environment to provide assistance to the users and to do maintenance work on the site.

Finally, the people working on the project need to be committed to seeing it succeed. Roger estimated that at TEAM a timeline of five years from the initial commitment to the finished product was reasonable.

In order to guide users through the software, we developed the following learning structure:

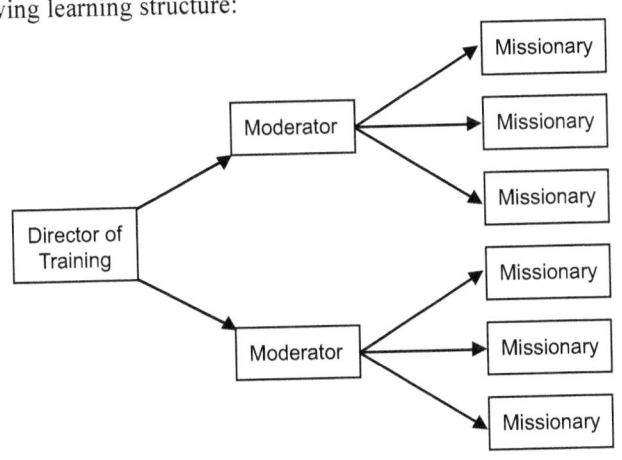

The director of training is responsible for overseeing all that takes place within the training environment and reports directly to TEAM's executive director. The moderators, who help the missionaries through their learning objectives and guide the learning groups, are responsible to him.

After assembling the team, the next step is to determine, as far as possible, where potential pitfalls lie. By doing this early in the process, the group is able to factor these challenges into their overall training strategy. At TEAM one of the most significant challenges uncovered was how to connect the training program to the missionaries who had poor Internet connections or who worked in countries where access to specific Web sites is blocked or monitored by the government.

To deal with this, a learning system was put together that could function as an online offering, but it could also be downloaded or burned to CD, and thus function without a Web connection. This meant making several modifications to the software package to allow the learner to be involved in the learning experience without having to be online. By using batch uploads and downloads, learners are able to stay relatively current in the discussions and interactions of the group without having to check in as regularly. An archival feature was also integrated into the training program that allows users to download and work through previous training modules on their own.

In order to accommodate the mobility of TEAM's missionaries—as well as the geographic dispersal of the people and churches it plans to bring into its training program later—TEAM structured it around learning communities. Learning communities are groups of people who have agreed to study a particular topic together. To a large degree, managing these groups can be done through a simple learning management system that is run from the home office and deployed via the Internet.

Considering who the users will be and how they will move through the training system should also be part of the strategic process. This includes determining how users will move from the inquiry process, through registration, and to the learning experiences, feedback, and final reporting. Will all of the learning participants be a part of the same organization? If not, who will the others be? Will there be any differences in the services between the two groups? If you will be charging a fee for learners to participate, this is also a good time to consider how you will do your billing and to figure out how your fee structure will work with your learning structure.

To answer these questions, it is worthwhile to spend some time researching what other businesses and ministries are doing about these issues. The group at TEAM responsible for developing online training found great ideas and suggestions in online white papers published by a variety of e-learning companies and by talking to schools that had already successfully developed and deployed an online learning component.

Software and Hardware

Making a good software decision is critical. It is the software itself that either facilitates or blocks an educational philosophy from being implemented. Software and hardware are both the means for developing the online training software and the constraints that define its limitations. Depending on the structure, goals, content, registration, and billing needs of your online learning program, you may choose anything from a full-featured learning management system from a large company, such as Blackboard, to a free solution that functions as a modified bulletin board, such as Nicenet (www.nicenet.org).

To get a feel for how online learning works and what resources are available, it is helpful to look at what other companies and organizations involved in online learning are doing. The American Society of Training and Development (ASTD, www.astd.org) is a great resource. Other helpful resources are the white papers published by Cisco (www.cisco.com) and IBM (www.ibm.com) on e-learning.

As agencies explore their options, they will find a number of different pricing strategies used by software vendors. Two of the most common are:

- **Seat licensing.** This works like a subscription service. The purchaser pays a fixed amount for the software itself and then is charged, based on the number of users.

- **Package pricing.** Package pricing often comes with higher-end software and allows the user to select and pay for only those features that he wishes to have as part of his software package.

It is also important to examine the costs associated with upgrading the software, particularly if it must be customized to suit the organization. Many software vendors have developed their learning software for the specific needs of a particular market. As a result, modifying or reconfiguring the software may be necessary. Depending on the pricing strategy of the vendor, this can cause problems when the time comes to upgrade the software. Consider whether the software has been designed for an instructor-led format or for peer-to-peer learning. Finding software that mirrors, as closely as possible, the strategy you have developed will help to keep your software modifications to a minimum.

Software maintenance and the amount of computer literacy required of the users should be weighed against the cost of a piece of software. Maintaining a program for ten users may work well, but it may become overwhelming when there are one hundred. Providing better helpdesk service for a smaller group of users in exchange for limited software capability may be fine initially but may prove to be a hindrance when the user base grows. A decision needs to be made about whether more expensive software will pay for itself in terms of money saved on support issues in the future.

Development and Prototyping

When the group has been formed and the software chosen, the next stage is developing and prototyping how the learning groups will function and how the software will be configured to support your objectives. While this is underway, it is a good idea to start the marketing and publicity campaign. By doing this, you will be able to build interest in the product, and you may be able to generate enough interest to smooth the launch of the learning program. This will be explained in more detail in the next section.

At TEAM the prototyping and development stage has taken significantly longer than was initially anticipated. However, the process has generated some valuable insights. Through the prototyping, some challenges were unearthed that would have remained undiscovered until the program went live, and there was opportunity to address them before they threatened to discourage users.

The team knew in advance that face-to-face communication is much different than communicating via the Internet. However, during the prototyping stage some specific discoveries were made, including the following:

- An active moderator must be involved in all learning groups to keep the learning community from stalling.

- All communication related to learning needs to take place in the learning software. When this does not happen, the group stalls as people begin checking other e-mail accounts for messages relating to learning.

- Good helpdesk support is essential in getting new users acquainted with the system and in working through software difficulties.

- Even if people do not communicate, it does not mean that they are not learning, though they may be feeling guilty or frustrated about their progress.

- While running trial learning groups, we found that occasionally people would drop out of the learning group. When we asked what had happened, we found that, in many cases, they had fallen behind and were embarrassed by their lack of progress. However, in some cases they continued to work on the learning goals on their own after the course was over.

- Getting started is the hardest part. For many users, even those familiar with computers, logging in to an online classroom or learning space and making their first posting is intimidating. Some users, afraid of posting something in the wrong part of the site, refrained from posting anything at all. As a result, the learning space stayed empty. To prevent this, moderators must begin the learning experience by posting in all areas of the learning space, demonstrating both how to post and what information to post in each place.

Developing a good user interface is another part of prototyping. As mentioned earlier, many online learning software packages have been developed for a specific market. Frequently, labels can be changed to use language that your users will find more intuitive. At the same time, there may be features that you would like to modify, add, or delete from the existing software. Most online learning software allows users some flexibility in making these changes without extensive coding.

Finally, the software needs to be tested before it is ready for launch. Testing should involve running several different scenarios and people other than the training team. People unfamiliar with the software and the goals of the learning are able to provide objective feedback on their learning experiences. This feedback should be taken into account before launch. Effective test groups should include people with varying computer experience to uncover flaws in the software. Making sure that the software works as smoothly as possible before launching the product is critical to its long-term success.

Marketing and Publicity

As stated above, marketing should begin during the testing stage to prepare the learning software for launch. The goal of marketing online training is to build enough demand for the product to start smoothly and gain the interest of your intended audience. This is important because launching a learning group that involves the participants requires that there be enough participants to maintain a steady flow of interaction. If there are too few, communication stagnates, and the learning groups will struggle to hold the interest of those involved.

At TEAM marketing began by developing a Web site organized around the promotion of the organization's lifelong learning core value (LifeLearner, www.lifelearner.net). This site provides general information about what the learning group is trying to accomplish, and what its mission, goals, and objectives are. Additional introductory information is also provided about how the learning groups will be set up. The point of the site is to provide ongoing information about the learning environment up until the point that the program itself is released.

Marketing needs to be targeted at the learners who will be using the software. Whether these people are inside your organization or outside, it is important that you show them the benefits of being involved in the learning experience you are developing, before the software is complete.

In TEAM's case, because of the geographical diversity of the organization, a marketing campaign was developed that began by using viral, or word-of-mouth, marketing. This meant spreading the concept and benefits of the learning groups to key people who would then pass them on to the group of people they spent time with, who would continue the pattern. This type of marketing has been popularized in a book by Malcolm Gladwell entitled *The Tipping Point*. The campaign started by contacting key leaders both inside and outside the organization and inviting them to join a pilot learning group where they could see the process from the inside and make suggestions for improvement.

This proved very effective in building interest as well as motivating those leaders to tell others about the program.

Other marketing strategies came from a PBS *Frontline* show called "The Merchants of Cool." This documentary shows how trends make it from the fringe to mainstream and are eventually seen as "cool" by the teen culture. It can be viewed online at http://www.pbs.org/wgbh/pages/frontline/shows/cool/. The online interview with MTV's Todd Cunningham, featured in the documentary, is especially insightful.

Depending on the scope of your training efforts, marketing may also take place outside the organization. To market to TEAM constituents, the upcoming training program was mentioned in as many in-house publications as possible. A constant effort was made to convince senior leadership of the importance of the learning program to the organization as well as to the many members. This meant showing how online learning fit into the strategic goals of the organization, how the learning structure could be used to communicate with key groups of people within the organization, and the benefits the program could provide as TEAM worked with supporting churches, foundations, colleges, and universities.

In spite of the importance of marketing to help ensure that there is enough interest and sufficient participation for a smooth start, the marketing must not oversell the capabilities of the learning program being developed or underestimate the amount of time it takes to produce it. Doing so risks eroding the interest and support gained during the marketing campaign.

Conclusion

Online learning provides an excellent way for an organization to develop its members and provide them with a way of sharing organizational knowledge across boundaries of space and time that might not otherwise be crossed. It provides avenues for leadership to use to communicate important information about the organization's goals and structure.

Developing an online learning program is a complex endeavor. It is costly and requires considering not only today's needs but also the needs the organization may face in the future so that they can be incorporated into the learning structure already in place. Getting feedback throughout the process from the various people involved in implementing the program is important because the content of the learning system as well as the software itself will have to be able to change to meet the expectations of the learners over time.

For this reason, decisions made at the beginning regarding educational philosophy and how to encode that philosophy in software are critical.

Care must also be taken not to lose sight of the fact that online learning is not the final word in organizational training, but simply the newest application of technology to the training process. Looking to it to solve all organizational training needs is to expect too much. But a careful application of the technology can provide great rewards for organizations looking to provide another avenue of training for their members.

JOEL DYLHOFF has been involved in organizational training and development and works as a Web developer, small business owner, and freelance writer. He has experience setting up online training and has written help documentation for an online learning environment.

11
Innovation in Theological Education in Africa
Paul Heidebrecht

Perhaps no book published in this new century has jolted evangelical readers as much as Philip Jenkins' *The Next Christendom*.[1] The world religions scholar from Penn State University has put the numbers on the table, and it's hard to avoid his conclusions.

The concept of Western Christianity is no longer of much value. Christianity is primarily a non-Western religion. In the decades ahead, the worldwide church will be dominated by the explosive church in Africa and the African diaspora. The church of the Southern Hemisphere will be young, nonwhite, poor, female, and theologically conservative, Jenkins predicts. Western academics have missed this global revolution and hardly realize how irrelevant much of their analysis has become. Even North American evangelicals, whose missionary efforts in the last two centuries are one of the causes for this massive demographic shift, have hardly grasped the significance of this Reformation-type change.

The fact is that it no longer makes sense to speak of a missionary-sending North America and the rest of the world as a mission field. There are almost as many missionaries being sent by African churches as there are coming from the West into Africa. Evangelism and church planting in Africa are occurring at a far more vigorous pace than anything North American missionaries ever enjoyed. Ironically, the largest church in Europe today is said to be one begun by African missionaries in the Ukraine.

Jenkins is not the only one to urge the removal of Western blinders and take another look at the church on continents like Africa. According to *Operation World* data, there are now more Christians in Africa than in North America (380 million in Africa compared to only 235 million in the United States and 24 million in Canada—these numbers measure membership affiliation and assume nominalism on both sides of the Atlantic). The Catholic Church, the Orthodox, and the major Protestant bodies are all larger in Africa than in North America.

One of the most successful evangelical mission agencies of the twentieth century, SIM (formerly, Sudan Interior Mission, now called Serving in Mission), established churches in Africa that now total more than nine million members. These African churches have sent and are supporting over one thousand cross-cultural missionaries across Africa and into Asia. Former SIM general director Jim Plueddemann attributes this phenomenon to "a noncontrolling, interdependent discipling relationship with national churches" pursued by the mission "so we can partner together to reach places neither of us could reach on our own." It's all part of what Plueddemann calls "a gracious revolution" in our thinking about world missions.

Nor are Westerners the only ones who need to take another look at Africa. Trinity International University's Tite Tiénou suggests that even Africans must change their language of missiology: "The most important missiological training in Africa is to liberate African Christians from perceiving themselves solely as recipients of mission." Kenyan missiologist Henry Mutua requires his students to research an African pioneer in missions. "There is an extensive literature on white Western missionaries," he says, "but very little on the Africans who took the gospel all over the continent."

To appreciate this maturing African missionary leadership, North American evangelicals need to become more familiar with the church scene on the continent. They need to discern the Holy Spirit's movement through this burgeoning church and be more personally engaged with its leaders.

One helpful window to this panorama of church and mission activity can be found in one of Africa's premiere theological schools, Nairobi Evangelical Graduate School of Theology (NEGST), the subject of this chapter. Admittedly, this is a small window. NEGST is only one of over one thousand theological schools and Bible colleges across Africa, though one of the more well developed at this point. But the faculty, students, and graduates of NEGST are representative of the growing edge of mission-minded churches in sub-Saharan Africa.

Furthermore, the relationships that North American churches and mission agencies are cultivating with schools like NEGST are demonstrations of Plueddemann's gracious revolution and suggest what this new century holds for evangelical churches in the Southern and the Northern Hemispheres. This chapter will describe several significant developments at NEGST that illustrate innovations taking shape in Africa.

The Story of NEGST

Begun in 1983 on a farm outside Nairobi, Kenya, by the fledgling Association of Evangelicals in Africa and Madagascar (AEAM, later changed to AEA), NEGST was a bold attempt by evangelical church leaders from numerous countries to launch graduate-level training for its pastors and teachers. NEGST was established for Anglophone Africa and Bangui Evangelical School of Theology (BEST) in the Central African Republic for Francophone Africa.

The visionary behind these two schools was Nigerian Byang Kato who helped form AEAM and who believed African Christianity would not survive without biblically grounded and theologically equipped leaders. Kato's accidental death in 1975 deprived this young evangelical movement of his forceful leadership. The two schools did manage to get off the ground despite limited resources and the practical challenges of transportation and communication. Every project in Africa is an act of faith from start to finish, and this is certainly the case with NEGST.

From the beginning the administrators and faculty of NEGST saw their new school as the place for preparing pastors for larger urban churches and teachers for the Bible colleges and schools across the continent. It took almost two decades to build a suitable campus and recruit a faculty that could match their ambition, but NEGST has managed to attract students from more than a third of Africa's fifty-five countries. Their faculty of over twenty-five is distinctly international with a core of African professors, all with earned doctorates. Trinity, Fuller, and Westminster are well represented among these scholars. Many of the African professors are editors and contributors to the *Africa Bible Commentary* and certain to be a sign of an emerging African evangelical theology.

The student body surpassed four hundred in 2005. This growth is partly due to classes being conducted off-campus in Nairobi churches and consolidating courses on Mondays for the benefit of full-time pastors. Many students live on campus with their families. Spouses enroll in certificate and diploma programs. Most students are already serving congregations and ministries and have numerous opportunities waiting for them upon graduation. Over five hundred graduates since 1986 have found their way into a wide range of church leadership roles on the continent.

The emergence of NEGST and BEST actually coincided with several other initiatives, such as a theological journal to encourage African scholars to write and a Sunday school publishing venture called *Christian Learning Materials Centre*. Kato argued for both of these in the 1970s as well as an accrediting association to set standards for African theological schools. A network of African church leaders and British and American missionaries took up the task after Kato's death and gradually made progress on all of these projects.

The Accrediting Council for Theological Education in Africa (ACTEA) was established in the early 1980s to ensure excellence and to be a tool of constant renewal for theological education. Interestingly, NEGST itself did not receive its accreditation from ACTEA until its twentieth anniversary. This work on accreditation may have been as critical as all the others simply because it compelled an ongoing dialog about what and how theological schools should be teaching and what their relationship to the church should be. That conversation should be occurring on every continent.

Developing Local and Global Missionaries

The missions department at NEGST currently enrolls more students than any other and is led by four outstanding missiologists—one Ethiopian, one Korean, and two Kenyans. Alemayehu Mekonnen states that their goal is "to blend piety, scholarship, and missionary service" and that they will sharpen, focus, and prepare any students who come with a passion for lost humanity and a sense of call to mission service.

Many of the students who come to NEGST are church planters who have recognized their need for more training and a deeper knowledge of the Scriptures. Few seem to have any sense of waiting for missionaries to come from other parts of the world but, rather, speak as if it is entirely their obligation and their joy to move across the continent and preach the gospel and start churches. The student council at NEGST initiates its own mission projects to other countries, sending students to preach and teach. Some students are even looking abroad to places like Europe, where thousands of Africans have settled, and are considering missionary service there.

Not all North American mission leaders have come to terms with the fact that African church leaders are not only sending out missionaries but are also training and equipping them to do missions well. But many have and some are responding in creative ways. The Evangelical Free Church of America's mission board has created several mission chairs at theological seminaries around the world, including NEGST, to be filled by national missiologists and is encouraging their churches to consider supporting these faculty positions.

Urban Missions

A third of Africa's population now resides in cities. For most urban dwellers, this means slums. Overwhelming every city are vast stretches of makeshift housing with limited water supplies and few public services. People survive under these conditions despite all the health risks and unemployment. In Nairobi 70 percent of the population can be found in the slums. But so can the church be found in the slums, lively and growing.

A significant number of NEGST students are pastors of slum churches or believe God has called them to this work. They acknowledge this will likely mean poverty for them as well since slum churches can hardly afford to pay their pastors. Spouses often work to support their husbands who care for congregations of the poor.

Henry Mutua teaches urban missions at NEGST and takes students into the slums and to the church where he does pastoral work.

For some students who have come from rural areas, it is eye opening. Those who have given themselves in service to slum churches speak of the emotional toll on themselves and recognize that pastors need to be nurtured. For many, their years at NEGST provide that refreshment of soul and body.

Mutua pays attention to urban ministry models in North America and keeps up with the literature. But he knows that African cities are different, not just because of the vastly deeper levels of poverty and the absence of any government support, nor because of the devastating AIDS epidemic. Urban Africans still maintain ties to their rural and tribal homes and live in two cultural worlds. Christians are always negotiating the demands of modernity and traditional African values, which probably makes them more effective cross-cultural missionaries than Westerners. Churches are often the only stable, trustworthy institution in African societies, and they have an incredible opportunity to impact the cities of the continent.

Islamic Studies

On no other continent of the world do Islam and Christianity confront each other on relatively equal terms. There are about 324 million Muslims on the African continent compared to 380 million Christians. Both are growing at a similar pace and both are seeking to claim the continent. Only in two countries, Nigeria and Sudan, has there been ongoing violent clashes between Muslims and Christians, though there are numerous other countries where tensions are mounting. With the obvious aid of oil money and zealous Muslim leaders from the Middle East, Islam in Africa has become much more assertive. Mosques are being erected everywhere, and in numerous countries, Muslims are pressing for legislation based on Koranic law. Yet many African Muslims have inherited a religion they barely understand and which they have fused with their traditional cultures.

NEGST theologian James Nkansah argues that friendship is still the best mission strategy and that through dialog Christians can help Muslim friends examine their religion and even what the Koran says about Jesus. Missions professor Mekonnen, on the other hand, believes churches need to be far more aware of Islam as a cultural and political force, which is why he launched an Islamic studies program at NEGST. He recruited two faculty members who earned doctorates under Fuller Theological Seminary's Islamic scholar, Dudley Woodberry. Students with a particular determination to do evangelism and church planting among Muslims are finding their way to NEGST for some of the best training available anywhere, and they are not all Africans either.

African Christians have not forgotten that the northern tier of Africa was once the stronghold of Christianity, producing such church leaders and theologians as Athanasius, Tertullian, and Augustine. Christianity was actually African before it became Western. But the church was supplanted by Islam, and North Africa remains a Muslim stronghold to this day. The failure of churches to adequately instruct their members in biblical knowledge and practice and to root the gospel in the many cultures of North Africa is viewed by some as a reason for Christianity's demise and a warning for African churches in this century.

While the primary focus of mission planning in Africa is on Muslim communities, NEGST students and graduates are also engaging the Asian-Indian populations in cities like Nairobi. There are over one hundred thousand Hindus living in the city, and church planting is occurring with them in mind.

African Bible Translators

Despite heroic efforts by Western Bible translators during the past century, Africa continues to be a continent with a majority of languages still lacking the Scriptures. Of the two thousand languages spoken on the continent, only four hundred have all or part of the Bible available. Close to another four hundred are being tackled, and at least three hundred more have been identified as worthy of translation work. The task is monumental and beyond the capacity of Western mission agencies.

African church leaders are stepping up to the challenge. In 1994 NEGST entered into partnership with SIL International to train linguists to take up the work of Bible translation. Over fifty students have graduated since then with a master's degree in translation studies and have been assigned to various countries to work. Some are even translating the Scriptures into their own mother tongues.

So important is this effort that NEGST started a doctoral program in biblical and translation studies in 2005. One reason for this step is the obvious need for future professors at NEGST and other theological schools in Africa who will train Bible translators and scholars in the decades ahead. NEGST will be one of the first evangelical schools in Africa to offer a doctorate. The school hopes to attract high-quality scholars who will do research and learn in the context of African realities such as poverty, AIDS, corruption, and the spirit world. The long-term goal is to produce another generation of African teachers and church leaders to guide the church on the continent and to take their place at the forefront of the global church.

Younger Independent Churches

Considerable attention has been given to the rise of independent churches in Africa in recent decades. Many identify themselves as indigenous African denominations with no connection to the West. Others are Pentecostal and linked to the growth of Pentecostalism around the world. It is hard not to notice these young churches in the cities of Africa. The worship style of their members is colorful, emotional, energetic, and often very public. They certainly help convey the impression of an exploding church across Africa.

Researchers like Jenkins point out that the Catholic Church and the Anglican Church are still far bigger than the independents and, in fact, are absorbing the practices of independent churches to hold on to their members and continue to grow. Church historian Andrew Walls believes "the distinction between older and independent African churches will in time become meaningless."

Leaders of younger independent churches tend to rely on a personal sense of direction by the Holy Spirit and God's personal call to engage in missions. They tend to mistrust theological education. This is true of many Pentecostals as well. But as these churches mature, biblical training and theological reflection become more desirable.

NEGST has begun to receive students from these churches. One student, Esther Obasike, came to Kenya with her husband, Prince, to plant Redeemed Christian Church of God (RCCG) congregations. The RCCG is one of the fastest growing denominations in Africa and has spread to eighty countries from its beginning in Nigeria in 1952. Congregations can even be found in six North American cities. After starting twenty-four churches in Kenya, Esther enrolled at NEGST to earn a degree in missions and become more equipped to fulfill her calling.

One of NEGST's trustees is Wilson Badejo, the general overseer of the Foursquare Gospel Church in Nigeria, a denomination begun by North American evangelist Aimee Semple McPherson and whose African membership now dwarfs that in North America. Badejo leads an aggressive church-planting movement in Africa but allies himself with schools like NEGST because of his concern for trained pastors.

Nonformal Education

The North American seminary has been criticized for its frequent failures to prepare pastors for the real life of the church and for its isolation from the church by its subjection to academic priorities. The theological schools in Africa are subject to the same criticism, partly, because they have followed a Western schooling model. Most of their administrators and faculty have been trained in Western institutions and assimilated their ethos and habits. Accreditation standards, while seeking to adapt to their cultural context, are also forced to accommodate to international requirements for scholarly work. Thus theological schools in North America and in Africa struggle to overcome the barrier between school and church.

In 2000 NEGST entered the field of nonformal education seeking to serve the church more directly by establishing an Institute for the Study of African Realities (ISAR). This residential study center located on its campus gave NEGST a means of offering church leaders a place to learn, dialog, resolve conflicts, research, and plan. Groups and individuals from many African countries have been guests at ISAR. The study center has also been a means for students to encounter African church leaders and to explore ways of dealing with social and moral issues facing churches.

Some of the impetus behind the study center was the recognition that most African pastors will never be able to obtain graduate-level theological education. They lack the financial resources and the academic qualifications. For most pastors, Bible school and extension courses of various kinds will be the only formal training they receive. The study center represents a form of continuing education that can be extremely profitable because it capitalizes on the actual issues pastors are facing in their churches and their communities. Experience, if properly processed, can be a valuable teacher. The study center at NEGST was designed to provide that kind of learning.

The study center functions as an alternative model of education where learners take more responsibility for their own learning and assist each other in learning as well as listening to resource people. Skeptics will say there is no escape from credentialism. Students of all ages are motivated primarily by grades. Certificates and degrees are tickets to better jobs, and so learning is secondary to doing what a school requires to receive their diploma. Even if this is true for many students, the study center at NEGST holds great promise for dialog among church leaders and students on critical issues that, in one way or another, affect how missions will be done in Africa.

Responding to the New Relationship

Anyone observing a school like NEGST and interacting with its students and faculty cannot help noticing their initiative for missions. The rising generation of African church leaders is moving out on all fronts, confident in the power of God, not intimidated by the prospects of poverty and persecution, believing that Africa and the churches are blessed with vast resources and potential. North Americans are inclined to view Africa as "hopeless." Fortunately, African Christians have more hope and more faith and possibly even more skill in taking the gospel across cultures.

The challenge for missions-minded North American churches is how to relate to the new demographics of the global church. It's easy to continue on with old paradigms and not even realize how irrelevant some of our efforts can be. The tragedy, of course, is the waste of our resources and the loss of opportunity to learn and grow ourselves.

In 2002 mission leaders of an older American denomination with a successful missions history were confronted by their international church partners with a simple request: help us develop our leaders. Instead of sending a youth group to do a work project or supporting another North American missionary, help us with student scholarships. Help us improve the quality of our theological schools. NEGST would make the same request.

For many North American churches, missions is about what *they* do or whom *they* send. A gracious revolution means asking the church around the world what it really needs. The priorities of the African, Asian, and Latin American churches must become factors in determining our global involvement.

Interestingly, most African church leaders are not opposed to more missionaries from the West. Indeed, some feel North Americans have abandoned them for more exciting places like China, the Muslim world, and the former Communist countries. But the missionaries Africans will welcome are those who listen more than they talk and who are seeking opportunities to minister together. Such missionaries will be encouraged to stay for a long time. There is still plenty to do on the African continent to accomplish the Great Commission, but North Americans will need to get more comfortable being guided by African leaders.

Patterns of Partnership

Fortunately, numerous examples of comfortable partnerships abound everywhere. NEGST enjoys many with churches and mission organizations in North America and Europe, as do other theological schools in Africa. Several interesting patterns in these relationships can be discerned.

One is the rise of laypersons with technical skills as short-term missionaries. Computer trainers and technicians are the most obvious. Several churches have created computer mission teams and sent them to NEGST to install equipment and train staff and students. Others have sent an individual or family. Librarians and building contractors and supervisors are also valuable missionaries welcomed at NEGST. Some stay for several years; others come for several weeks at a time over many years. Ted Ward calls them "a new species" in missions—tentmakers, moonlight missionaries, and contracted specialists.

A second pattern is churches cultivating personal relationships with faculty members. A number of the African faculty at NEGST enjoy long-term friendships with one or more churches in the United States and, on occasion, visit these churches. These relationships may have begun when the faculty member was a graduate student in the United States and attended the church, or it may have started as a result of a visit to North America when the professor preached or taught at the church. If North American churches are serious about listening to African church leaders, they must be willing to listen to Africans preach from their pulpits and teach in their classes. Financial support may or may not be part of this relationship, but at least some African church leaders (or Asian or Latin American) should be part of a church's missions family.

Third, supporting students with scholarships continues to be a popular and effective way of investing in future African church leaders. Almost all students at schools like NEGST need scholarship help. This is equally true in North American seminaries where tuition fees represent only 25 percent of the total income for most schools. Donors heavily subsidize all seminaries wherever they are. At NEGST many donors initiate contact with the students they are supporting and follow them through school into their church ministry. School administrators have learned that these scholarship programs have to be managed properly with clearly stated expectations for both the donor and the student and maintained with regular communication to donors. They have also learned that they need to spend time in North America visiting churches and promoting scholarships for their students.

Lessons Learned the Hard Way

In its first two decades, NEGST has also experienced its share of difficulties with North American friends. Partnerships between North Americans and Africans are clumsy affairs at best. Cross-cultural training can minimize blunders, but it cannot protect us from all our mistakes.

The most common misunderstanding is over the use of funds given by churches and individuals to an institution. Many donors give with a specific project in mind and expect to see tangible results. School administrators at institutions like NEGST face financial crises frequently and have to make agonizing choices over which obligations to fulfill

Innovation in Theological Education in Africa

first. It is not unusual for contributions to be used different from what donors are assuming. The only way to avoid these frustrations is to engage in constant, open conversation about projects and financial need and policies of the school. North American and African partners have to understand what the other is experiencing in the relationship and together find mutually satisfying ways to work together on a project. There are no shortcuts, only the requirement to engage with each other.

North American church members have the resources to travel to Africa and visit schools like NEGST. They should go. It's the best way to even begin to understand Africa and the church scene. Besides, a relationship is not complete until both partners visit each other in their homes. But many visits to Africa by North Americans turn out disappointing for the guests and the hosts. Often, this occurs because North American church leaders want to do in Africa what they do at home—preach and lecture and function as experts. Too often, these leaders assume their material and experience is equally relevant in an African context, and their African hosts are too polite to tell them it is not. Even North American seminary professors can fail to adapt their courses to what little they know of the African church.

A wiser alternative is to go as a student, not a teacher, and to ask questions and observe. Don't speak any more than is necessary. This alternative will require some gentle educating of North American churches that like to send their members on mission trips so they can be missionaries. Trips can certainly include some organized activities by the participants but should also include plenty of time socializing with and listening to African church leaders and members.

In the end, relationships between North American and African church leaders fail simply because the relationship is not two-way and mutual. One party is helping and the other is being helped. Usually, North Americans are the ones doing the helping. Their need to be taught and challenged by Africans is not obvious to them. Nor do they seem to realize that North America is as much a mission field as Africa, and, possibly, even more. The day is upon us when African missionaries and churches and teachers should be welcomed and honored among us.

If the worldwide church is in fact becoming more southern and dominated by Africans and Asians and Latin Americans, then men and women graduating from and teaching at schools like NEGST are, in effect, our leaders, our teachers, and our missionaries.

PAUL HEIDEBRECHT is executive director of Christian Leaders for Africa, a nonprofit ministry that promotes theological education in Africa to churches in North America and represents NEGST (www.clafrica.com).

Conclusion

12
The Next Generation of Innovators

Jim Reapsome

Mission history includes both peaks and valleys. Some people think that world missions started with William Carey (1761–1834). This idea suggests that nothing much happened between the sending of Paul and Barnabas by the Antioch church (Acts 13:1–3) and Carey. It's as though the story of world missions leaps from the Antioch peak to the Carey peak, with only a huge, 1,700-year valley in between.

Historically, of course, Christianity spread both East and West, to India, China, and Japan as well as to Western, Northern, and Southern Europe and Africa and Latin America. Many missionary innovators made this possible. This is neither the time nor the place to recount their exploits.

Arbitrarily, then, we start with Carey, who deserves to be acclaimed the father of modern Protestant missions. (In this account we limit ourselves to Protestants, but academic integrity requires us to acknowledge the significant achievements of Catholic missionaries as well.)

We'll call Carey the first modern mission innovator. He published the first global survey of world missions in 1792. He went to India in 1793 and served forty-one years in Bengal without a furlough. Among a host of other innovations, he translated and printed the Bible in thirty-five languages.

Imagine what he could have done had he had available the kind of technological breakthroughs in Bible translation and publishing described in Jon Hirst's chapter. Modern innovators follow Carey's lead, trying to make the Scriptures more readily available in compatible formats to more and more readers.

The early nineteenth century produced organizational innovators who started the London Mission Society and the British and Foreign Bible Society. In 1806, without any church or mission agency sponsorship, students at Williams College (Massachusetts) held what became known as the Haystack Prayer Meeting, which birthed several denominational foreign mission boards.

They provoked the same kind of fresh thinking described by Ellen Livingood, Brent Lindquist, Joel Dylhoff, Paul Heidebrecht, Jon Hirst, and Kurt Wilson. They had no precedents to follow, no organizational ties. They simply followed the Holy Spirit's promptings and broke down the establishment's reasons for doing nothing to take the gospel to non-Christian peoples. That seems to be the pattern of mission innovators. They sense a need, find a niche to fill, and move ahead in the spirit of the old Haystack Prayer Meeting.

The real explosion in missionary innovations came later in the nineteenth century and on into the early years of the twentieth century. The fuse was lit by the Student Volunteer Movement, which had the audacity to adopt as its watchword, "The evangelization of the world in this generation." Evangelist D. L. Moody spearheaded this movement. Being the innovator that he was, he was not content to hold evangelistic campaigns. He looked beyond the cities of North America and Europe to the vast reaches of the world where people were dying without ever hearing about the Lord Jesus Christ.

Moody not only had the dynamic—he had the creativity and the energy to move people to act in world missions. So did a host of other missionary innovators, women as well as men. Just to name a few: J. Hudson Taylor (1832–1905), Lottie Moon (1840–1912), Samuel Zwemer (1867–1952), David Livingstone (1813–1873), Mary Slessor (1848–1915), Rowland V. Bingham (1872–1942), C. T. Studd (1862–1931), Adoniram Judson (1788–1850), Robert Jaffray (1873–1945), and Amy Carmichael (1867–1951).

These people innovated in China, Africa, Burma, India, and the Muslim world. They are among the mountain peaks because they dreamed new visions, broke traditional stereotypes, and exhibited courage and faith to accomplish what they knew was God's will. Today strong churches thrive in places where they sowed the seed of the gospel.

Innovators also stirred the churches and college campuses. Among them were John R. Mott (1865–1955), Robert E. Speer (1867–1947), A. B. Simpson (1843–1919), and Fredrik Franson (1852–1908). The peak of this outpouring of missionary enthusiasm was reached at the great 1910 Edinburgh world missions assembly.

Similarly, in more recent times, innovators convened InterVarsity's student missions conferences at Urbana, Illinois, which produced thousands of new missionary recruits from 1946 onward. Other modern innovators inspired milestone gatherings at Lausanne, Switzerland (1974), Singapore (1989), and the AD2000 and Beyond movement.

The tide of missionary obedience swelled before World War I but ebbed in the 1920s, 1930s, and 1940s for a number of reasons, including theological liberalism in some denominations. The staggering Hocking Report in the early 1930s claimed that the era of missionary work was finished.

But after World War II, the old missionary passion was rekindled, bringing a host of new innovators who radically changed the face of world missions. Among them were: Arthur Glasser, Louis King, Kenneth Strachan, Frank Laubach, Cameron Townsend, Joy Ridderhof, Clyde Taylor, Francis Steele, John Stott, Philip Armstrong, Robert Evans, Ralph Winter, Robert Pierce, Bill Bright, Donald McGavran, George Verwer, Brother Andrew, Philip Hogan, Peter Wagner, Bruce Wilkerson, Moishe Rosen, Loren Cunningham, Luis Bush, John Kyle, David Howard, David Adeney, Festo Kivengere, Francis Sunderaraj, Tokunboh Adeyemo, Tite Tienou, Patrick Johnstone, Thomas Wang, Jun Vencer, Warren Webster, Jim Montgomery, and Greg Livingstone.

Not all of them produced new missionary organizations as did Cameron Townsend (Wycliffe Bible Translators), Robert Pierce (World Vision), Bill Bright (Campus Crusade for Christ), Moishe Rosen (Jews for Jesus), Donald McGavran (School of Church Growth at Fuller Theological Seminary), Loren Cunningham (Youth With a Mission), Brother Andrew (Open Doors), Joy Ridderhof (Gospel Recordings), George Verwer (Operation Mobilization), Greg Livingstone (Frontiers), and Jim Montgomery (Disciple a Whole Nation). Other innovators opened new vistas that led to new strategies and new ways of considering the church's mission. For example, Patrick Johnstone's monumental research compiled in *Operation World*[1] probably has called more people to pray for world missions than any other vehicle.

This is not meant to be a hall of fame of innovators, for good reason: many innovations come not from conspicuous leaders but from women and men in the trenches who figure out new ways of attacking old problems. They do not start new mission boards but quietly work within existing agencies to bring about reform and change. They adapt strategies to local needs and circumstances, some of which are widely accepted while others fail to gain notoriety.

It's also interesting to see how some things we call innovations in our time were actually put to wide use in the late nineteenth century.

Long before tentmakers pushed their way to the forefront of mission strategies, early missionaries to the Muslim world had to find ways of acceptance by deeds of charity and social service—such simple things as teaching women to sew.

Nevertheless, we have to mention certain other relatively recent mountain peaks that qualify as innovations. In this list we include the spectacular rise of so-called Third World mission agencies. These sending boards have arisen by the hundreds across Asia, Africa, and Latin America. Thousands of women and men from South Korea, Singapore, the Philippines, India, Nigeria, and Brazil, for example, have crossed cultural boundaries with the gospel.

To this we must add the phenomenal growth in both tentmakers and short-term workers. Roger Peterson's chapter provides in-depth understanding for the rise in the numbers of short-termers.

We have also witnessed remarkable innovations in relief and development work and Jewish evangelism. Church-planting efforts have been redoubled in hard-to-reach places, identified as the 10-40 Window. This concept (the countries east of 10 degrees longitude and south of 40 degrees latitude) captured the imagination of hundreds of churches, which decided to focus on sending new missionaries to these never- or least-evangelized people.

Other innovations of the last half of the twentieth century included Evangelism-in-Depth campaigns in Latin America, New Life for All campaigns in Africa, Christ the Only Way campaigns in the Philippines, and Discipling a Whole Nation efforts in Asia and Africa.

Innovations were introduced in community-based health care, literacy campaigns, theological education by extension, the *Jesus* film, Evangelism Explosion, the CoMission effort when the former Soviet Union opened, the use of ships by Operation Mobilization, prayer warfare walks, and concerts of prayer.

Meanwhile, significant innovations came in the twentieth century from the scholarship and writings of such people as Roland Allen,

Innovation in Mission

Rufus Anderson, Henry Venn, John Nevius, Stephen Neill, Hendrik Kraemer, Peter Beyerhaus, J. H. Bavinck, George Peters, Harvie Conn, Donald McGavran, J. Herbert Kane, David Hesselgrave, David Bosch, Robertson McQuilkin, Samuel Escobar, Tite Tienou, and Ajith Fernando. Each one gave missionary practitioners much new food for thought and stretched them to think about the mission task in fresh ways.

We must also acknowledge the innovations in technology that have greatly enhanced the spread of the gospel. We start with the printing press (c.1450) and race on to photography, radio, television, motion pictures, satellite broadcasting, audio and videocassettes, telephones, faxes, computers, aircraft, and the Internet. These are the kinds of innovations discussed by our writers in earlier chapters.

Taking all of these innovations together, we marvel at their worldwide impact for the cause of Jesus Christ and his church. Despite the fact that the twentieth century may go down as the bloodiest of all time—for all people as well as Christians—we see churches growing rapidly today in places where all hope seemed lost. We need only to look to China, South Korea, and the former Soviet Union and Eastern Europe as prime examples.

Secular historians already have written that the most significant innovation of all at the close of the twentieth century was the dynamic church and missionary growth in Africa, Asia, and Latin America, which John Maust describes in his account of the authors and publishers developing and creating much needed resources. Non-Western believers and missionaries now outnumber those from the North and West.

Just reviewing the last fifty years or so requires us to wonder what surprises God has for us in the next fifty years. Can we expect as many innovators and innovations to come to the forefront of missionary thought and practice between now and 2050? Why not?

The Next Generation of Innovators

That thought may either terrify or encourage us. Of one thing we can be sure: God's missionary program will never stand still. Someone will come along with a better mousetrap, so to speak, and many people will be buyers. We have tried to introduce some of those new concepts in this book.

On the other hand, we can also be certain that innovators and innovations will be opposed by the inflexible people, those who say we've always done things like this before. If we could talk to some of the innovators listed above, they would tell us of many difficulties and obstacles they faced from within their own ranks. I knew some of them personally, and I know how hard they had to fight. I sat on some of their boards and heard the arguments back and forth, sometimes for years, before new ideas were accepted.

That will not change. Whether in the world of science, medicine, or missions, innovators are not often received gladly.

We know that our technological capabilities will not stand still. We have to be ready to use whatever new tools God brings our way.

Another thing in favor of innovation is the rising tide of scholarship in world missions. Courses in mission studies have multiplied. Graduate studies in missiology have prospered. Scholars and missionaries and the heads of agencies are finding new ways to cooperate and learn from each other. Out of such magnificent resources as these are bound to arise future innovations.

Looking back also reminds us how God had put his sovereign hand on certain people. He just called them to innovate and they answered. We cannot identify such people in advance. God does this because world missions is *his* program, not ours. He cares more about world evangelism than we do. Our hope for the next fifty years is based on the certainty that, even now, he is putting his hand on women and men, not just in the United States, Canada, and Europe but also in Latin America, Africa, and Asia. From their ranks will come tomorrow's innovators, people like Ah Kie Lim, Sam Chiang, Aaron Sandoval, and Joseph Vijayam whose works you have read in this book.

We have also seen how churches have risen to the innovations of the last fifty years. As new missionaries have come forth, churches have increased their budgets accordingly. Some churches have become their own sending agencies. Others have set strategies of their own and have worked with existing boards. Mission pastors have been added to church staffs. Church budgets also include funds for technological advances and the training of students in seminaries around the world. Churches have been quick to support short-term teams.

Will churches continue to invest heavily in world missions in the future? Costs are rising in some places. Demands on the home budget—including new building programs—threaten the levels of financial support.

But money is not the only hurdle the churches have to overcome if we are to see innovations adopted and supported in the future. Lack of strong prayer support could easily detract from future effectiveness and so could the lack of a firm biblical foundation for world missions.

The innovators cited above tell amazing stories about how God answered prayer and opened doors so they could step out in faith. People believed in the cause and prayed mightily for it to succeed.

Young women and men now stand on the threshold of greatness and new adventures in God's world missions program. They will look to their churches to give them the green light to pursue their vision and their dreams. Some of them we have already noted in this book. We can only pray that in the years to come, God will keep on giving us new ways to bring the good news of Jesus to many more people and to build up those who need training to be better pastors, shepherds, and teachers.

This book is a brief panorama of what we see coming on the horizon, highlighting certain technological innovations as well as strategic innovations in a number of areas. Many more will be shaping the world of missions tomorrow. Stay in touch through the new blog established by Generous Mind: http://www.generousmind.com/communities.php

---

JIM REAPSOME was the founding editor of *Evangelical Missions Quarterly* in 1964 and edited the journal until his retirement in 1997. He was executive director of Evangelical Missions Information Service, Wheaton, Illinois, publisher of the quarterly, and editor of *World Pulse* from 1982–1997. His book *Final Analysis* is a compilation of his editorials in *World Pulse*. He has also served as the managing editor of *Christianity Today* and as a pastor in Pennsylvania. He is a graduate of Franklin and Marshall College and Dallas Theological Seminary. He is the author of numerous Bible study guides published by InterVarsity Press, Zondervan, and Waterbrook Press. He has been adjunct professor at Trinity Evangelical Divinity School and also taught missions and journalism courses at Columbia International University. He has served on the boards of InterVarsity Christian Fellowship, Latin America Mission, Greater Europe Mission, Interact, Media Associates International, Arab World Ministries, and Manara Ministries in Amman, Jordan.

Notes

Preface

1. The Lausanne Covenant was written at the First International Congress on World Evangelization. This conference was headed by Billy Graham and was held in 1974 in Lausanne, Switzerland. The Covenant was drafted by John Stott to outline the essential nature of the gospel and the importance of evangelizing. It was agreed upon by 2,300 people from 150 nations from all branches of the Christian church in the space of ten days.

Chapter 2: Innovation in Kingdom Business

1. J. Christie Wilson, *Today's Tentmakers* (Wheaton, IL: Tyndale, 1980), 28–35.

Chapter 3: Innovation in Member Care

1. Belinda Ng, "Some Reflection on Pastoral Care," *Too Valuable to Lose: Exploring the Causes and Cures of Missionary Attrition*, ed. William D. Taylor (Pasadena, CA: William Carey Library, 1997), 280.

2. Kelly O'Donnell, ed., *Doing Member Care Well: Perspectives and Practices from Around the World* (Pasadena, CA: William Carey Library, 2002).

3. Kelly O'Donnell and Michelle O'Donnell, "Perspectives on Member Care in Missions," *Missionary Care: Counting the Cost for World Evangelism*, ed. Kelly O'Donnell (Pasadena, CA: William Carey Library, 1992), 13.

4. K. Rajendran, *Which Way Forward Indian Missions? A Critique of Twenty-Five Years: 1972–1997* (Bangalore, India: SAIACS Press, 1998), 108.

5. Ah Kie Lim, "Field Care for Asian Missionaries in South Asia," *Doing Member Care Well: Perspectives and Practices from Around the World*, ed. Kelly O'Donnell (Pasadena, CA: William Carey Library, 2002), 88.

Chapter 5: Innovation in Training Writers and Publishers

1. Philip Jenkins, "The Next Christianity," *The Atlantic Monthly* (October 2002).

2. Judith Markham, *Servanthood and the Christian Editor* (Bloomingdale, IL: Media Associates International, 2003).

3. Patricia Vergara, *La Aventura de Escribir* (Lima, Peru: Ediciones Puma, 2003).

Chapter 6: Innovation in Content

1. Richard Tiplady, *World of Difference* (Carlisle, UK: Paternoster Press, 2003), 117.

2. Jeremy Rifkin, *The Age of Access: The New Culture of Hypercapitalism Where All of Life Is a Paid-for Experience* (New York: JP Tarcher-Putnam, 2000), 14–15.

3. Lynn Upshaw, "Building an Internal Marketing Program" (//http: www.brandbuilding.com/best/buildinginternal.html).

Chapter 8: Innovation in Strategic Planning and Partnerships

1. China watchers do not have a definitive number, only God does. The range runs from 14 million to 70 million claimed by some groups. For example, an article in *ChinaSource*, Spring 2003, suggests the number at the lower end, but another article in *Evangelical Missions Quarterly*, April 2000, suggests a figure at 40 million.

2. *Educause Review* 40, no. 3 (May–June 2005): 40–53; Yazhou Zhoukan 2006/01/15; http://news.bbc.co.uk/2/hi/programmes/click_online/4586914.stm, Friday, 6 January 2006.

3. Samuel Chiang, "Serve. Assist. Partner: How to Help the Church in China Meet the Challenges of a New Generation," *Evangelical Missions Quarterly* (January 2002); "The Greatest Need in the Chinese Church," *ChinaSource* (April 2003).

4. The written Chinese language in China is the "simplified script." In Taiwan and Hong Kong they use the "traditional script." There were plenty of "traditional script" Bible programs but none in "simplified script." Furthermore, the double-byte coding did not translate well from traditional into simplified codes. Today under "Unicode" standard, this knotty issue has shrunk.

5. Two decades ago, I had served with Ernst & Young in the Canadian national office and worked with a team that released software for internal use (in Canada, U.K., U.S.A., and Bermuda).

6. Today Microsoft has become the dominate force, but the Chinese government is pushing for the Linux platform, so as to diversify its risk.

7. I had formerly served with Partners International from 1991–2001.

8. Though I used the word *organization* here, I do mean to encompass the local church, which, in many ways, can, and often does, function as an organization.

9. Chuck Bennett was formerly CEO of Mission Aviation Fellowship International and Partners International; he was also a recipient of the Peter Drucker Award for CEO Excellence.

10. Dr. William D. Taylor, executive director of the Missions Commission, World Evangelical Alliance, has been a mentor from a distance for the last 15 years.

11. Dr. Dennis Mock was the founder of Biblical Training Center for Pastors in Atlanta, GA.

12. Dr. Daniel Ma, Dr. Patrick So, Rev. Stephen Chan, Mr. Lim Sip-Li (a world-class photographer from Singapore who provided photos and descriptions with tie-ins to the Old Testament and New Testament Scripture), Source of Light Ministries, Biblical Self-Confrontation, and others God provided.

13. Dr. Stephen Olford (1918–2004) was a champion of expository preaching and a mentor to many evangelical leaders. He founded the Stephen Olford Center for Biblical Preaching in Memphis, TN. Born in Zambia as a son of missionaries, Olford hosted the weekly radio show "Encounter," heard on Christian radio stations in the United States, Canada, and overseas.

14. God has allowed both forms to exist, and Christians outside of China tend to pick one form over the other. But in creating a mass-media software tool, one must embrace the church.

15. Bill Smith is a Trainer of Strategy Coordinators for the International Mission Board of the Southern Baptist Convention (SBC). Lewis Abbott served as a pastor for over forty years in the SBC, and is currently with the National Christian Foundation.

Notes

16. "Challenges Facing China's Church Leaders Today," *ChinaSource* (Summer 2001). China has the world's largest concentration of youth: 631 million are under the age of 24.

17. Wu Yi was the Health Minister in China.

18. A partial list includes: U.S.A., Canada, Costa Rica, Brazil, Peru, Panama, Uruguay, Holland, England, France, Poland, Norway, Kenya, Ghana, South Africa, Ivory Coast, La Reunion, Madagascar, Russia, Kazakhstan, Kyrgyzstan, Israel, Egypt, Turkey, Nepal, India, Thailand, Vietnam, Philippines, Malaysia, Myanmar, Cambodia, Singapore, Taiwan, Hong Kong, Macau, Japan, Korea, Mongolia, China, New Zealand, Vanuatu, Fiji, and Australia.

19. Music by Handel, 1747; words by Edmund L. Budry; translated by R. B. Hoyle.

Chapter 11: Innovation in Theological Education in Africa

1. Philip Jenkins, *The Next Christendom* (Oxford University Press, 2002).

Chapter 12: The Next Generation of Innovators

1. Patrick Johnstone and Jason Mandryk, *Operation World: When We Pray God Works* (WEC International and Paternoster, 2001).

www.ingramcontent.com/pod-product-compliance
Lightning Source LLC
Chambersburg PA
CBHW070546170426
43201CB00012B/1741